LEADERSHIP

Leadership

HUDSON · T · ARMERDING

Tyndale House
Publishers, Inc.
Wheaton, Illinois

LIBRARY OF CONGRESS CATALOG CARD NUMBER 78-64673
ISBN 0-8423-2126-8, CLOTH
ISBN 0-8423-2125-X, PAPER

FIRST PRINTING, NOVEMBER 1978
PRINTED IN THE UNITED STATES OF AMERICA

To my wife Miriam
whose walk with the Lord
has immeasurably enriched
our life together

CONTENTS

PREFACE

FROM GODLY PARENTS I learned the value of regular, reflective reading of the Scriptures. In the providence of God, opportunities for the ministry of his Word have been a further encouragement to explore the text and meaning of the Bible. My perspectives were expanded through years of experience in the Armed Forces and in higher education as well as in the Christian ministry. All of these elements have combined to bring into sharper focus the viewpoints contained in this book. These have been shared from time to time in the Wheaton College chapel and at retreats in east and west Texas. The presentation at the Officers' Christian Fellowship conference center in Colorado, however, was the occasion that prompted Lieutenant Colonel Arnold Sanderlin of the Fellowship to suggest this volume. He and Mrs. Mary Buker, who typed the manuscript, deserve special credit as do the staff of the College, particularly my secretary, Mrs. Virginia Lassen, and my associate, David L. Roberts.

CHAPTER ONE
MINORITY STATUS
John 15:11-21

ANYONE CALLED OF GOD to Christian leadership should recognize that he or she will be working with a minority in our society. Awareness of the meaning of our minority status is essential to effective leadership. This awareness is sometimes achieved best through a vivid experience.

For my training as a U.S. Navy midshipman in World War Two, I was assigned to a school that had taken over some of the facilities of Columbia University in New York City. When we had time off, we trainees often went to the Times Square area, which was not then in the condition it is in today. Thanks to the excellent subway service, we had no difficulty reaching that area, provided we knew which trains to take.

On one occasion I entered the subway to ride back to the University but I boarded the wrong train and ended up in Harlem. As I climbed up to the street level and started to walk back toward Columbia University, I found that I was the only white man in the area. In a tangible way, I sensed what it was like to be a racial minority.

In today's world evangelical Christians are a minority. We are like Abraham, who looked for a city. We are like those who followed him as strangers and sojourners in the earth. While evangelical Christians number approximately 40 million in the

United States, this is less than 25 percent of the more than 200 million who live in our country. Furthermore, within the total religious population of a little over 100 million in this country, we evangelicals still constitute less than 50 percent. So even in this instance we are a minority. But this is nothing new. God's covenant people in the Old Testament were a tiny minority among the nations of the world. Nor is there prospect of change. The parable of the sower teaches that there will not be a widespread acceptance of God's Word. Only a minority will respond to it.

Granted that this is so, we should recognize that we tend to react in a variety of ways to our being a minority. It is the responsibility of the Christian leader to be aware of these tendencies so as to give constructive guidance.

Sometimes our reaction to our minority status is to make ourselves comfortable in it. One of the most common ways in which we do this is to withdraw into a community that is distinctively evangelical. That seems to be a natural tendency that was true even of the first-century church. The believers at Jerusalem initially stayed together presumably because they enjoyed the fellowship of one another and sensed a security in their relationship. Yet the Lord did not permit them to remain isolated from the people around them.

The book of the Acts provides illustrations of how God counteracted the believers' natural tendency toward isolation. You can find the first illustration in the opening part of the eighth chapter—immediately after the stoning of Stephen. Scripture says: "And Saul was consenting to his death. And at that time there was a great persecution against the church which was at Jerusalem, and they were all scattered abroad throughout the regions of Judea and Samaria, except the apostles."

View this in light of Acts 1:8: "But ye shall receive power, after that the Holy Ghost is come upon you: and ye shall be witnesses unto me both in Jerusalem, and in all Judea, and in Samaria, and unto the uttermost part of the earth." The Lord's word would have been honored if his disciples had gone out without any further action on his part. But they didn't. So he used persecution to send believers into the regions of Judea and Samaria.

From Acts 11:19 we know that those thrust out in this way continued to extend their witness. The verse says, "Now they which were scattered abroad upon the persecution that arose about Stephen travelled as far as Phoenicia and Cyprus and Antioch preaching the word to none but unto the Jews only."

At this point the Lord so ordered circumstances that the extension would be more than geographic. This is described in Acts 13:44: "And the next sabbath day came almost the whole city together to hear the word of God. But when the Jews saw the multitudes, they were filled with envy, and spake against those things which were spoken by Paul, contradicting and blaspheming. Then Paul and Barnabas waxed bold, and said, It was necessary that the word of God should first have been spoken to you: but seeing ye put it from you, and judge yourself unworthy of everlasting life, lo, we turn to the Gentiles. For so hath the Lord commanded us, saying, I have set thee to be a light to the nations, that thou shouldest be for salvation unto the ends of the earth. And when the Gentiles heard this, they were glad, and glorified the word of the Lord."

Scripture goes on to say that the Jews stirred up the devout and honorable women, along with the chief men of the city, and expelled the witnesses who then came to Iconium. Here the process was soon repeated, as described in Acts 14:4: "The multitude of the city was divided: and part held with the Jews, and part with the apostles. And when there was an assault made both of the Gentiles, and also of the Jews with their rulers, to use them despitefully, and to stone them, they were aware of it, and fled unto Lystra and Derbe, cities of Lycaonia, and unto the region that lieth round about: and there they preached the gospel."

From these illustrations it is evident that God uses persecution to insure that his people do not grow comfortable in their minority status and retreat to what may become a Christian ghetto. I have had to keep this in mind in my home town. The city of Wheaton is humorously characterized as the Protestant Vatican or the Holy City because it is the headquarters for numerous evangelical organizations. Thus, Christians often have Christian neighbors. Local service clubs include a significant number of Christians in their memberships. Yet, periodically there is opposition by non-Christians. I believe one reason why God permits that opposition is to keep the Christians of Wheaton from becoming comfortable in their unusual environment, lest they fail to remember that God wants the evangelical minority to spread abroad to fulfill the commission that our Savior gave to his people.

A second factor in God's dealing with his people as a minority is illumination. An illustration of this factor is found in the tenth and eleventh chapters of the book of the Acts. The Apostle Peter had been faithfully proclaiming the gospel to the Jews only. While he was waiting to eat and was meditating on the housetop, he fell into a trance and saw a sheet coming down from heaven filled with various creatures. Then he heard a voice say, "Rise, Peter: kill and eat." Peter's response was: "Not so, Lord, for I have never eaten anything that is common or unclean." In reply the Lord said, "What God hath cleansed, that call not thou common." For emphasis this was repeated three times.

This threefold emphasis was not unique in Peter's experience. After he denied the Lord three times and was restored, the Lord three times over asked Peter if he loved him. Perhaps the apostle was so fixed in his convictions that he needed a repeated emphasis in order that he might not fail to understand what God was telling him.

What was the point of the sheet let down from heaven? It seems clear that it was that the gospel was not to be limited to the Jew only. By supernatural illumination, God indicated that the gospel of the grace of God was to be spread abroad among the Gentiles as well as the Jews. So in addition to persecution, God provides illumination to broaden his people's perspective. One should understand that in our time there is far less need for illumination of the kind given to Peter. In his day the Canon of the Scriptures was not complete, and thus he needed special instruction to impress upon his understanding just how universal the application of the gospel was to be.

There is a third factor, which may not be as easily understood. It is found in Acts 15, beginning with verse 36. This account illustrates the integrity of Holy Scripture in not omitting incidents that may reflect unfavorably upon the people of God. The passage reads, "And some days after, Paul said unto Barnabas, Let us go again and visit our brethren in every city where we have preached the word of the Lord, and see how they do. And Barnabas determined to take with them John, whose surname was Mark. But Paul thought it not good to take him with them, who departed from them from Pamphylia, and went not with them to the work. And the contention was so sharp between them, that they departed asunder one from the other: and so Barnabas took Mark, and sailed unto Cyprus; and Paul chose Silas, and departed, being commended by the brethren unto the grace of God. And he went through Syria and Cilicia, confirming the churches."

God has been able to use even differences of opinion such as this to fulfill his purposes in the spread of the gospel. Because Christians with honest disagreements form different fellowships, they tend to extend their respective ministries and thus make possible a wider dissemination of the gospel. While differences are regrettable, yet God is able to work for his glory in spite of our finitude.

Furthermore, some of us have different needs than others as we respond to the Word of God in worship and service. Some believers prefer a formal worship service, in which everything is prescribed in accordance with a pattern such as that found in the Book of Common Prayer. We appreciate the dignity and the sublimity of the words, and we find the symbolism

15

meaningful. Others of us are uncomfortable in that kind of service, precisely because it is so structured. We fear that our saying "Amen" at the wrong place in the service would annoy other worshipers. On the other hand, if those same worshipers went into a service where people said "Amen" frequently and all prayed audibly at the same time, they might also be uncomfortable.

So, while we may regret the divisions which human inadequacy causes and which pride perpetuates, we must recall that one of God's outstanding servants, the Apostle Paul, was in disagreement with another spiritually minded Christian, Barnabas. The two could not agree about taking a young man with them. On this issue they actually parted company. Yet I am convinced that through that turn of events the testimony of the Lord was extended in a more comprehensive way.

Finally, God uses an expanded perspective to overcome our natural provincialism. We see an instance of this in Acts 16:9: "And a vision appeared to Paul in the night; There stood a man of Macedonia, beseeching him and saying, Come over into Macedonia, and help us." This the apostle did.

In our day we seldom if ever receive such visions to help us overcome our limited outlook. Instead, we can gain this perspective through personal observation made possible by our opportunities to travel. Many of us have personally experienced this. For years, I had read about the spiritual need of India as evidenced by the dominance of heathenism and its pervasive control over the people of that country. But until I visited India and was taken by one of our alumni to a Hindu temple, I did not really understand the incredible spiritual bondage of those people. We watched beautiful Indian women bow down before an idol and cast flowers into a receptacle before it. From the expression on their faces, it seemed the worshipers were in agony as they implored the pagan deity to have mercy upon them. Even though I had read about the religions of India, my study was no substitute for the

16

experience of actually seeing the way in which these people were bound and how desperately they needed to be made free in Jesus Christ.

Our pastor at that time had the same experience. He reported seeing a little boy begging. His master had severed his forearms and legs so that he could move about only by crawling on his stumps. The amputations were done so that the little boy would evoke pity and thus get more contributions for the master. To the pastor this was unthinkable. He could scarcely imagine anybody being so cruel. He came back with an urgent desire to do something so that the preaching of the gospel might result in compassion for children such as that little boy.

Thus God may use travel or the information that comes from mission boards or films to give us a vision of the need for our involvement in the world in witness and service. Such a perspective can counteract our tendency to withdraw as a minority seeking only the security and comfort of our own group.

In contrast to withdrawal, we are sometimes tempted to be absorbed into our culture by being what some people have called the Christian secret service. In this way, nobody will know we are Christians. I heard of an incident that occurred when a Christian with this tendency went into a restaurant and bowed his head to give thanks for the food. As he did so, the waitress came over and asked him if something was wrong with the food. He was terribly embarrassed and made some excuse that he was just looking at his food to see if it was all right. He was unwilling to acknowledge that he was a Christian giving thanks to God for his meal.

What is it that can save us from being so absorbed into our culture that we become indistinguishable from the non-Christian? Certainly persecution has done this even as it made the Jews of Hitler's Germany clearly distinguishable from other Germans. There is also the prospect that awaits God's people, as seen in Hebrews 11. Verse 13 says, "These all died in faith, not having received the promises, but having seen them afar off, and were persuaded of them, and embraced them, and confessed that they were strangers and pilgrims on the earth. For they that say such things declare plainly that they seek a country." Then in verses 39 and 40 the Scripture says, "And these all, having received witness through faith, received not the promise: God having provided some better thing for us, that they without us should not be made perfect."

Besides allowing persecution, another way God keeps his people from being absorbed into the surrounding culture is to summon them to consider the prospect seen so clearly by the heroes of the faith listed in Hebrews eleven. Those heroes were not attracted to this prospect because things were easy for them or because they had status and temporal benefits in their position as Christians. Quite the opposite. The account says, beginning with verse 33:

"Who through faith subdued kingdoms, wrought righteousness, obtained promises, stopped the mouths of lions, quenched the violence of fire, escaped the edge of the sword, out of weakness were made strong, waxed valiant in fight, turned to flight the armies of the aliens. Women received their dead raised to life again: and others were tortured, not accepting deliverance; that they might obtain a better resurrection; and others had trial of mockings and scourgings, yea, moreover of bonds and imprisonment: they were stoned, they were sawn asunder, were tested, were slain with the sword: they wandered about in sheepskins and goatskins; being destitute, afflicted, tormented."

Within our American culture, it is difficult for us to grasp the impact of those people's experiences. Today if we have discomfort or pain or difficulty, we can usually take some kind of chemical comforter to ease the pain, even to the point of being so tranquilized that trouble and difficulty simply do not bother us. By contrast, God's people then were not shielded from these things. They did not have a just society. They did not get proper or fair trials. They were harassed and deprived.

They lost everything, including their lives—often in the most dreadful circumstances. Yet the Scripture says of these that they all died in faith, not having received the promises. What kept them going?

It was their faith. They believed that God's promises would eventually be fulfilled and that they would share in his triumph. That prospect kept them faithful even though to the natural mind nothing whatsoever would justify such faith. No doubt some urged them to renounce their faith so as to stop the torture and save their lives and their possessions. By way of response they might have said, "We have seen the Lord. We have accepted his Word. We believe that his promises will be fulfilled and we are willing to suffer any indignity and endure any persecution since we know that these promises are true."

What were some of the promises they had in mind? One of the promises had been given to Abraham. Hebrews 6 says, "And so, after he had patiently endured, he obtained the promise." What was this promise? It was that in him all the nations of the earth would be blessed. When he patiently endured and believed God, then he received the promise in Isaac. Both Abraham and the faithful who followed him believed that the blessing of all nations through Abraham's seed would surely come.

Consider also verse 17: "Wherein God, willing more abundantly to show unto the heirs of promise the immutability of his counsel, confirmed it by an oath: that by two immutable things in which it was impossible for God to lie, we might have a strong consolation, who have fled for refuge to lay hold upon the hope set before us: which hope we have as an anchor of the soul, both sure and stedfast, and which entereth into that within the veil; whither the forerunner is for us entered, even Jesus, made an high priest for ever after the order of Melchisedec." In the ninth chapter, beginning at verse 15, we are told that the promise of eternal inheritance is in our Lord Jesus Christ and in his redemptive ministry. Finally, in Hebrews 10:36 we see the promise of the coming again of our

Savior: "For you have need of patience, that, after you have done the will of God, you might receive the promise. For yet a little while, and he that shall come will come, and will not tarry."

What then is our prospect? It centers ultimately in the coming again of our Lord Jesus Christ and the establishment of his rule of righteousness and peace that will bring blessing to all who have put their faith and trust in him.

Those who are called of God to positions of Christian leadership should thus recognize their minority status and help God's people to be a creative rather than a regressive minority. They can so lead as they constructively respond to God's Word and his ordering of circumstances, ever keeping in view the biblical vision and prospect: "Even so, come Lord Jesus."

CHAPTER TWO
TROUBLE
Matthew 5:1-12

BESIDES RECOGNIZING THE MINORITY status of the evangelical community, the Christian leader must also accept the inevitability of trouble and difficulty. This is because the Lord Jesus said his people would experience such in the world.

You can receive trouble constructively. This is what the Apostle Paul had in mind when he declared, "We glory in tribulations also." The same emphasis appears in the Sermon on the Mount where our Lord declares we are blessed when we are subject to persecution. This is a point of view the non-Christian world can't understand. Yet it is consistent with other statements in Scripture. For example, the Lord says, "Whoever will save his life, will lose it, and whoever will lose his life for my sake and the gospel's will save it."

Such an assertion is absurd, says the puzzled non-Christian. And when you tell an unbeliever that it is a blessing to be persecuted, he may call you a masochist, psychologically abnormal to be able to rejoice in trouble. But this is why these biblical statements are addressed exclusively to the redeemed community who are informed by the Holy Spirit and are thus able to accept a biblical rationale that transcends the speculations of mankind.

It is to us believers, therefore, that the Lord Jesus speaks when he says, "Blessed are ye when men shall revile you and persecute you, and shall say all manner of evil against you falsely for my sake." Certain illustrations help us to understand what our Savior had in mind when he made this statement. Consider these from his own experience.

The first is described in Matthew 27 beginning at verse 39: "And they that passed by reviled him, wagging their heads, and saying, Thou that destroyest the temple, and buildest it in three days, save thyself. If thou be the Son of God, come down from the cross. Likewise also the chief priests mocking him, with the scribes and elders, said, He saved others; himself he cannot save. If he be the King of Israel, let him now come down from the cross, and we will believe him. He trusted in God; let him deliver him now, if he will have him: for he said, I am the Son of God. The thieves also, which were crucified with him, cast the same in his teeth."

This is an illustration of what our Savior meant when he said, "Blessed are you when men shall revile you." Notice the circumstances. The Lord Jesus is stretched out upon the cross. Because of the sovereign will and purpose of God he cannot come down; he must bear his suffering patiently. He does not respond even though his revilers concoct their accusations by taking specific statements and twisting them out of context.

With sardonic irony the crowd shouts that if he is the Son of God, he should come down from the cross and then they would believe him. In derision they call out that he saved others, but cannot save himself. Even one of the thieves who was being crucified with him urges that if he is who he claims to be, he should save himself and them as well.

This is one kind of treatment a Christian can expect. We will experience occasions when we will be unable to defend ourselves because of the sovereign purposes of God. Obedience to his commands will sometimes prevent us from responding. Statements made in integrity will be twisted and turned back against us. This is what is meant by reviling.

The Scripture also provides illustrations of what is meant by persecution. One example is particularly poignant. The Apostle Paul mentions it in the third chapter of Philippians where he uses the expression, "concerning zeal, persecuting the church." This is an allusion to what the book of the Acts tells about Paul's treatment of the church before he became a believer himself. In the last part of Acts 7 is the report of Paul's participation in the stoning of Stephen. Then in chapter eight is the account of how he entered the houses of Christians and saw to it that they were put into prison because they were believers in our Lord Jesus Christ. Scripture says that as he was on his way to Damascus, he was breathing out threatenings and slaughter. This is what is meant by persecution: invasion of privacy, removal of rights, denial of a fair trial. Thus what the Apostle Paul did to the church before he became a Christian gives us a scriptural illustration of persecution.

The third category of trouble is having all manner of evil spoken against us falsely, for Jesus' sake. For an illustration of this, consider again the experience of our Lord Jesus Christ as described in Matthew 26, beginning with verse 59: "Now the chief priests, and elders, and all the council, sought false witness against Jesus, to put him to death; but found none: yea, though many false witnesses came, yet found they none. At the last came two false witnesses, and said, This fellow said, I am able to destroy the temple of God, and to build it in three days." This was followed by the high priest's interrogation and his condemnation of our Savior through a misrepresentation of the evidence.

I suspect that after the disciples had seen the events leading up to the crucifixion, our Lord's statement must have come back to them with great force—especially to Peter, who had personally observed what took place. Thus it would not have been difficult for them to see how false accusers could be hired to discredit their testimony, even as it happened to their Savior.

23

In light of the Scripture, "Blessed are you when men shall revile you, and persecute you, and shall say all manner of evil against you falsely for my sake," we should ask two questions: Who are the persecutors and who are the persecuted? Are any of us being so persecuted?

In the original language, there is no specific word for men at this point in the text, and so the translators simply supplied the term as that which was implied. Certainly men do the actual persecuting, reviling and evil speaking. But I believe they are acting on behalf of a being who has set himself in opposition to the Lord, and to the Lord's people. That evil being is Satan.

You see an instance of this in the book of Job. When the various beings came before the Lord, Satan also came. The Lord asked him if he had considered Job. Satan had indeed done so but he knew the Lord was protecting his servant. At that point Satan received permission to afflict Job but spare his life. It is obvious that Satan did not directly inflict the catastrophes but used the weather, the Sabeans and the Chaldeans to bring about Job's suffering.

Opposition comes also through spiritual adversaries. I am thinking of an instance of such spiritual opposition in the book of Daniel (10:12, 13). Daniel had prayed but there was no answer. Then when the angel came he told Daniel that the Prince of the King of Persia had withstood him for twenty-one days. Who was the Prince of the King of Persia? I think he was one of Satan's emissaries who in the spiritual realm was doing battle with God's messenger. Recall also that Paul in Ephesians 6 tells us that our warfare is with "spiritual wickedness in high places."

I suggest, therefore, that when the reviling and the persecution and the evil and false statements come, Satan is directing this against the Christian and is using his children and various devices in an attempt to achieve his purposes. When our Lord Jesus was confronted with those who challenged his statements, he said that they were doing the deeds of their father, the devil. Thus there is an integral relationship between Satan and those who follow his direction in opposing the Lord and his people.

That is what makes our Lord's statement "for my sake" so significant. We are not important in Satan's eyes for our own sakes. We are really inconsequential to him. His only reason for attacking us is that we bear the name of Christ. Once we bear his name we become significant to Satan because we are then part of his enemy.

Now, we must ask whether we are the persecuted and whether our Savior's statement therefore applies to us. Certainly, for some Christians there is no doubt but that they have suffered persecution. Yet others have not had the same experiences.

I recall my first night as a seaman apprentice. When I knelt to pray by my bunk, other men walked by and kicked my feet and my legs. That made concentration difficult. In fact, I can't remember anything that I said to the Lord because I was so nervous. Even so, I was not really reviled. There was some ridicule, but nothing akin to what happened to our Savior. Furthermore, I have never had the experience of having my home entered, or of being arrested and put in jail for my faith. Nor have I stood trial and had false witnesses testify against me to convict me.

What then should we conclude? Did the Savior mean that his statement would apply only to a segment of Christians and only at particular times such as the Inquisition, or in selected locations in Mainland China or North Korea or some parts of Russia? I do not believe so. When we think of persecution, we tend to consider it to be visible, physical, and material. This is understandable, for the Bible describes such forms of persecution. The Lord Jesus physically suffered upon a literal cross. The people who accused him verbally shouted out their accusations and reproaches. The early Christians were actually taken from their homes and imprisoned. But are these the only ways in which Christians can be persecuted? You probably know by experience that the answer is no.

I know of a gifted man who was called of God to a ministry that was both creative and difficult. His church is at the intersection of two different communities. One is very impoverished; the other is counter-cultural, with much that is perverted and sinful. This man directed his ministry for the Lord toward both of these neighborhoods.

After a period of years a friend learned that the man was seriously considering leaving the ministry. He asked him why. The man told him he was overwhelmed with a sense of futility and despair. Therefore he thought the only honorable thing to do was to leave the ministry.

I recognize that about 15 percent of the population of our country suffer from depression. I know that both men and women reach a time in life that brings a major emotional and psychological change. But the way this man described his experience, it did not fit into either of these categories.

After listening to his description of his feelings, his friend called upon God to rebuke the enemy so that he would not have the advantage over this gifted and sensitive servant of the Lord. While the man was not being persecuted outwardly or physically, he was being terribly persecuted inwardly.

I have had an experience of that kind. It occurred during a brief study leave on a ranch in West Texas. Living alone in the old ranch house, I would work on manuscripts in the mornings and then go out in the afternoon to do ranching. Most of the time I prepared my own meals. After lunch one noon I was washing the dishes. All during the forenoon a disturbing memory had kept coming into my consciousness. It was a memory of something that had happened years before—an act of disobedience for which I was terribly ashamed. I had been convicted about that sin, had confessed it, and had sought by God's grace to forsake it and put it away. Yet that morning repeatedly the recollection of that experience kept coming back. It was like a constant accusation that would not cease.

As the forenoon went on, the situation got worse. By lunch

time I was in an agony of spirit because I knew the recollections were true. I knew that what was being said was accurate. But as I was bending over the dishes, suddenly this word came just as clearly as if someone was in the room: "If we walk in the light as he is in the light, we have fellowship one with another, and the blood of Jesus Christ, his Son cleanseth us from all sin" (1 John 1:7).

I knew that a more accurate translation would read: " . . . *continues* to cleanse us from all sin." Immediately, tears mingled with the dishwater because the Lord Jesus in mercy and through the Holy Spirit had reminded me of the unchanging truth of his word of forgiveness on the basis of his atoning sacrifice. Thus God overcame the persecution of Satan that was calculated to imprison me in guilt and to challenge the deliverance wrought by the Lord.

Such persecution is very real. I believe furthermore, that the more strategic your position is as a Christian leader, the more you will face this kind of persecution. As I have come to know Christian leaders, I have learned of similar experiences they have undergone. So the fact that people do not literally shout at us, or drag us off to prison, or bring false witnesses against us in a court of law, does not mean that the enemy is not doing exactly what the Lord Jesus said would happen to the Christian. His words in John 16:33 remain true: "In the world, you shall have tribulation."

Faced with the reality and the inevitability of persecution, how are we to understand "blessed are you"? It would be incomplete to say, "Blessed are you when men shall revile you and persecute you and say all manner of evil against you falsely for my sake," and stop there. Some might use this as an excuse for masochism. Indeed, some do suffer because of their own faults and sins rather than for Christ's sake. In such cases we cannot consider ourselves blessed but must recall the Apostle Peter's statement that if we suffer it should not be as an evil doer. Thus if we suffer, let us ask ourselves frankly whether it is for his sake.

If it is, we must keep in mind all that our Savior said. This provides both prospect and retrospect, to make our perspective complete. Both these elements—prospect and retrospect—are found in the words, "Great is your reward in heaven, for so persecuted they the prophets who were before you."

The retrospect to which I referred relates to the prophets who were before us. Many of them were persecuted for their faith. Within the context of Christian discipleship, it is appropriate to look at the example of others, because the Christian, as a redeemed person, has the capacity to respond to a creative example. This is consistent with the Apostle Peter's statement, "Christ also has suffered for us, leaving us an example that you should follow his steps . . ." The Christian can follow Jesus because the same life that is in him is in the Christian. Thus that life is able to act in a manner consistent with that of the Savior.

As members of the believing community the prophets who went before us also suffered, as described in Hebrews 11. This should encourage us and should save us from morbid introspection or childish self-pity. The prophets' experiences corroborate the Apostle Paul's statement that no testing touches us but that which is common to man. Thus we can rejoice and be exceeding glad when we realize that the saints and the martyrs of the past have been able to stand—and we can as well. They suffered; so can we. They endured; so can we. Thus we can give thanks that we are counted worthy to suffer shame for his name as did those who have gone before us.

The other factor is prospect, as expressed in the words, "Great is your reward in heaven." It does something to us to know that a recompense is coming. It helps us to endure the temptations, the testings, and the trials. It is good to know that the Lord Jesus will someday say to us, "Well done." Our Savior provides a poignant illustration of this in his reference to the woman who is about to give birth to a child. The reason she endures the pain of childbirth is that she knows she is going to have the privilege of welcoming a new life into the world.

When Carreen, our oldest child, was about to be born, I was a student at the University of Chicago. Because of that, my wife was admitted to the Chicago Lying-In Hospital, one of the finest in the world. The staff there allowed husbands to stay with their wives right up to the point of delivery. I did so and will always remember that experience with a sense of reverence and thanksgiving for my wife and for the miracle of new life being brought into the world. Ever since that day, I have understood much more fully what our Savior was saying. He encourages each of us to recognize that if we encounter difficulty or pain or agony, beyond it is our great reward in heaven. So we are to rejoice and be exceeding glad.

The Christian leader should certainly have this perspective and should encourage others to share it as well, both by exhortation and by exemplification. Then the believing community will be able to confront tribulation with both gratitude and blessing.

CHAPTER THREE
INTERDEPENDENCE
1 Corinthians 12:14-27

A SIGN IN THE OFFICE of a businessman says: "Bloom where you are planted." This should be true of the Christian. By his grace God has called each one of us to salvation. Our Lord Jesus Christ said that no one could come to him unless the Father who is in heaven would draw him. And so each of us has come because of the gracious provision of God to call us to himself.

What we may not realize, however, is that God sovereignly calls us not only to salvation, but to vocation. This is not understood by some Christians. They apparently feel that only a segment of the Christian church is called of God into specific areas of service. Thus, believers are classified as clergy and laity—dividing us into those called to serve God and those who decide for themselves what they will do in life. Such a distinction is not biblical. Scripture teaches that every Christian has a God-given ministry to perform in the place of the Lord's choosing.

One of the key Scripture passages dealing with this subject is 1 Corinthians 12. Two major emphases emerge in this chapter. One is that God in his sovereignty locates each of us within the structure called the body. The other is that we have a personal responsibility as part of that body to act as God has ordained that we should.

First, let us consider the fact that God has placed each of us in the body where he wants us. This means that God calls us to our vocation as part of his purpose and plan for his people in the world.

Some years ago my wife and I applied for service under the China Inland Mission, now called the Overseas Missionary Fellowship. I had been in the Pacific theater during World War Two. We were married during the war. Then it seemed to us that God was calling us to return to the Pacific area to serve him as missionaries in China. Thus, following my discharge from active duty I went to the University of Chicago to prepare to minister to students of China.

In China's traditional social system the scholar was at the top of the scale. Our thought was that if we could reach the students, we would influence leaders who would then reach many others for Christ. We felt that this would be the best way for us to use our time and energy in presenting the gospel of Christ and the witness of the Word of God to the people of China.

In 1948 we went to missionary candidate school and were accepted by the mission. Because we were expecting our second child, we could not go overseas immediately. A year later we applied for a visa, but the State Department refused to grant it because conditions were too hazardous in China. We were in a dilemma. We were sure we had been called to China. We were ready to leave. But now the door was apparently closed. With agony of soul we asked the Lord what he would have us do.

It was then that I happened to meet R. E. Thompson, who had been with the China Inland Mission and who was then with Missionary Internship. I explained our problem to him. In response he asked whether we were prepared to do the will of God, whatever it might be. I said that we were. Then he asked whether we had submitted our mind to the Lord so that he might show us his will. Again I answered in the affirmative. At that point he asked what opportunity was open to us. I replied that the president of Gordon College, where we had been teaching, had invited us to return to work there. He surprised me by saying we should take that offer. When I protested that we were called of God to be missionaries, he went through the series of questions again. Then I saw the point.

I learned then that God calls us to a *vo*cation, but he does not necessarily limit this to a particular *lo*cation. In other words, we were not restricted to serve the Lord only in China, but we were called to serve students. Ever since 1946 we have been involved in ministry to college students. And even though other opportunities have come our way from time to time, God consistently has kept us in the student world. So we have concluded that God called us to our vocation even though the location differed from what we thought it would be.

We should keep in mind, however, that changes in location are part of God's strategic plan for his work in the world. I remember one occasion during World War Two when our ship was ordered out on a search and destroy mission against some Japanese units. We were detached from the main body and steamed for several hours. Then we received word from the admiral to turn around and steam back again. To some of us junior officers this seemed a senseless waste of time and money. Later we found out that Japanese ships had been coming in to intercept us. Had they done so, we probably would have been sunk. Knowing the circumstances, the admiral ordered us back for our own safety. Similarly, God knows what we do not or cannot know and has his own strategy. Consistent with his strategy, he locates his people where he wants them—sometimes for safety, sometimes to engage in battle, sometimes even to be killed.

Typically, two different reactions to God's strategy are often advanced. The first of these is the popular notion that the individual Christian is of little consequence to the work of God. No doubt you have heard people say they are only businessmen, or only tradesmen, or only housewives. Yet Scripture says (NIV), "If the foot should say, 'Because I am not a hand, I do not belong to the body,' it would not for that reason cease to be a part of the body. And if the ear should say, 'Because I am not an eye, I do not belong to the body,' it should not for that reason cease to be part of the body." By the Holy Spirit the Apostle Paul is emphasizing here that our perception of ourselves is not necessarily consistent with God's strategic use of us. We may say, in effect, "I am a foot, and because I am not a hand, I am not part of the body." Thinking that way does not determine whether or not we are part of the body.

In the fall of 1972 Wheaton was playing a football game with Millikin University in downstate Illinois. We had a player on our team named Wayne Wray. As we kicked off to Millikin, Wayne ran downfield and tackled the ball carrier. At the same time another player also tackled the carrier. The ball carrier and the other man got up, but Wayne remained stretched out on the ground. The trainer, the doctor, and the coach all ran onto the field, and in a few minutes they realized that Wayne's injury was very serious. They rushed him to the local hospital for emergency treatment. Later they learned that the bones of his neck had moved so much that he might have been instantly killed. Finally Wayne was taken home to Springfield, Massachusetts. Eventually he was able to be up and around again, but he was confined to a wheelchair.

In June 1975, Wayne's class, which was now graduating, brought him back to campus for commencement. He came to the platform in his wheelchair. On that Commencement Day it would have been inconceivable for one of his classmates to tell him that feet really did not matter. With conviction he would reply that they do matter. How this former athlete would like to race down the field again! But he cannot. He must sit in a wheelchair. Through his difficult circumstance he has learned how important his feet were to him. He knows how absurd it would be for feet to say, "Because I am not another part of the body, I am, therefore, not part of the body."

We know a lovely girl from Korea named Kim Wickes. Kim was blinded in an accident. Later she came to the United States for musical training. She has an outstanding memory so that she can hear something once and remember it. She sings without benefit of sheet music, and has an extensive repertoire.

Kim attended the International Congress on World Evangelization in Lausanne. Cliff Barrows introduced her and she sang, "His eye is on the sparrow, and I know he watches me." I thought I was the only one crying until I looked around me. All those on either side of me were overcome with emotion as well. As this young lady sang, she profoundly blessed us all.

Suppose you were to ask Kim, "Does the ear not being an eye mean that it does not belong to the body?" She would of course tell you just how definitely she needs her ears. She must have her hearing to be able to minister in music. She needs her hearing also in order to recognize people and respond to them. Kim cannot consider the ears unimportant. And wherever God puts each of us we should seek to function normally so that the body of Christ may be organically whole. Each of us is as important to the body of Christ as ears are to Kim Wickes and as legs were to Wayne Wray.

An illustration from one of C. S. Lewis's works is helpful at this point. In *That Hideous Strength,* a head was being kept alive by artificial means. It was supposed to be the focus of attention and of reverence; yet it was a horrible, misshapen mass that really had no capacity to function at all. It had no body to which it could issue orders. If we were all to be detached as unnecessary, the bodyless Head would be as much a monstrosity as the head in that C. S. Lewis book. But God calls us to a vocation as part of his strategy in the total working of the body of Christ.

The other way in which God's sovereignty is questioned is the opposite of claiming insignificance. It is to declare that we can get along without the rest of the body. The Scripture comments on this as follows (NIV): "The eye cannot say to the hand, 'I don't need you!' And the head cannot say to the feet, 'I don't need you!' On the contrary, those parts of the body that seem to be weaker are indispensable, and the parts that we think are less honorable we treat with special honor. And the parts that are unpresentable are treated with special modesty, while our presentable parts need no special treatment."

Suppose a hungry man comes in to a table to eat a meal. Before him is a steak done to his liking, a baked potato broken open, with melted butter flowing down its sides, and the vegetables done to perfection. Then suppose his eyes say to his hand, "We don't need you." In reply the hand says, "Since you don't need me, that is your problem." Without the help of the hand the eyes could desire the food with great intensity, but would never get it from the plate to the mouth unless the hand was there to do it.

The same thing is true where the feet are concerned. The head might realize that there was danger in being on a railroad track with the train coming. Without the feet to carry the body to safety, there would be no escape.

When we think of the body of Christ, we may doubt that a gifted theologian needs anyone to help him. But does an executive need bookkeepers, maintenance personnel, computer operators and such like? Common sense tells us he certainly does. The problem with some of us in Christian leadership, however, is that we on occasion come to the place where we really believe we do not need other people whom we certainly do need.

From painful experience I have learned the necessity of taking steps to overcome this tendency. At the college several years ago I organized what became known as the president's council. It was composed of senior administrative officers. I told them that it was not a suggestion but an order that they were to be completely straightforward with me because I needed their perspective and insight in dealing with college matters. At the outset they may not have been entirely sure that this was really what I wanted, but after working together for a while they seemed to feel free to question or to disagree.

This is not to imply that my responsibilities are now shifted to them. I do not believe that the head should say, in effect, "I couldn't help myself. They made the decision for me." That would be an abdication of responsibility. But when others share their perceptions and insights, the head can make better decisions. For this to occur, however, the leader must be sincere in seeking the viewpoint of others and must not be unduly defensive.

An incident in a military staff meeting of senior and junior officers illustrates what I mean. One of the senior officers told the group to feel free to comment on the policies they were to discuss that day. A young major responded by courteously but clearly pointing out what the policy limitations were. As he was finishing, one of the senior officers got up and said, "Shut up and sit down." Obviously what was said at the outset was not really meant. Instead the junior officers were expected to agree with whatever the senior officers thought was appropriate.

In the body of Christ, on the other hand, there ought to be enough personal security on the part of those who have the responsibility to lead, that they can receive criticism and differing viewpoints without reacting defensively. Otherwise, we are saying in effect that we do not have need of others.

If we would apply this biblical principle more generally, we would suffer far fewer mistakes and wrong decisions. In my judgment, some disasters in our country were due at least in part to the fact that some of our leaders were not willing to listen and that some of the subordinates were not willing to state their opinion when it was desperately needed.

Dr. Harold Ockenga, for years the pastor of Park Street Church in Boston, Massachusetts, has shared an illustrative experience out of his own life. He told of a lady in the city of Boston who scrubbed floors for a living, and who prayed for him every day. Her praying was one reason his ministry was effective. Dr. Ockenga has a gifted mind and an unusually deep understanding of the Scriptures. Yet he realized that part of the reason God made his ministry fruitful was not because of his towering intellect or his strategic location at Park Street Church or his ambition to do things for the Lord, but because that lady who scrubbed floors held him up to the throne of God. Although she did not have his intellect, she loved Jesus Christ and supported Christ's cause by praying that he might be used of the Lord.

Very often, when we pray for others we do so because they are experiencing a terminal illness or a moral lapse or some other crisis. Certainly we should pray for people in such situations, but we should also pray for those who seem to have everything, who are very successful, and apparently have need of nothing. Beneath the facade of the self-confident, seemingly fully self-contained individual, are great needs. One of the most critical of these needs is for the ability to handle success properly. Unfortunately, far too many leaders have been ruined by success. Among the vital ministries of one part of the body to another, is the ministry of prayer for the successful ones.

As we recognize the truth that we are each placed by God in our special ministry within the body of Christ and that we need one another in Christian fellowship, let us also note another major emphasis in 1 Corinthians 12 (NIV): "God has combined the members of the body and given greater honor to the parts that lacked it, so that there is no division in the body, but that its parts should have equal concern for each other. If one part suffers, every part suffers with it; if one part is honored, every part rejoices with it."

This suggests an important area of our responsibility because God has combined us so that we might have no division, but equal concern for each other. We should not forget that it is pleasing to God for us to rejoice when his will is done, no matter who gets the credit. God's ideal for the body of Christ is for both the followers and the leaders to keep his will paramount in their ministry one for another and in their concern for each other.

This is sometimes difficult to do. If we have worked hard

and then someone else gets the credit, a feeling of resentment can easily arise. We may feel like the lineman on a football team—we open the holes but the backfield players get the glory. We argue that if the holes had not been there, the backfield would never have made a gain. Many of God's people are linemen who help the backfield to go through.

It is easy for people in Christian leadership to acquire "backfield" reputations if it is not clear that any ministry is to be one of service, not of domination. Rather than boasting about jurisdiction over others, a real leader should adopt the point of view voiced by the man promoted to a high position, who said, "Now I can serve more people." If you as a leader can realize that your major task is to minister to your subordinates so that they can find complete fulfillment through your oversight and direction, then you will succeed well in your role within the body of Christ.

Such an outlook can radically alter your view of your subordinates. No longer are they a threat. No longer do you feel uneasiness if they get credit. Rather you experience delight in seeing them fulfilled and successful. When you enable your subordinates to be successful in their work you are obeying what our Lord Jesus Christ said to his disciples: "Whoever will be chiefest among you, let him be servant of all."

Where Christians have genuine concern one for another, the subordinates pray for the leader that he will be able to handle success properly and that he will have what is necessary for his work. The leader meanwhile will see that his followers find fulfillment in their work. In so doing he will manifest what our Lord Jesus Christ said should characterize those who would be chiefest of all—the servant of all whom he would seek to lead.

CHAPTER FOUR
EXAMPLING
1 Timothy 4:12-16

In his first letter to Timothy the Apostle Paul exhorted his son in the faith to be an example of the believers. In connection with that exhortation, Paul also indicated several categories in which Timothy (and we) should exemplify faithful believers. The Christian leader in particular is responsible to be this kind of example. Thus it is important that we cultivate those characteristics that will give tangible evidence of our commitment to Jesus Christ as Lord and Savior.

Furthermore, as the apostle indicated to Timothy, leadership is more a matter of quality than of seniority, even though Scripture urges respect for age. In God's economy, merely living longer does not necessarily qualify an individual for leadership. A tragic illustration of one whose leadership became increasingly *defective* as he grew older is the Old Testament priest, Eli. In contrast, inspiring illustrations of young but effective leaders are easy to find in both Testaments. Thus, those who are younger should not be reluctant to cultivate qualities of leadership, recognizing that in the biblical context youthfulness is not synonymous with immaturity.

One of the church fathers, Irenaeus, indicated that in Timothy's time the term youth referred to those up to forty years of age—perhaps because so many leaders at that time were much older. So Timothy may possibly have been forty years of age.

I understand that a study of those listed in *Who's Who in America* showed that a significant number of them gained their reputation when they were young people. This does not rule out the possibility of a Grandma Moses or a Colonel Sanders who gained acclaim after the age at which most others had retired. It does suggest, however, that the apostle's word of encouragement to Timothy can be taken seriously in Christian circles today as well.

The Christian leader should understand the biblical use of the term *example*. In the language of the New Testament it has the basic meaning of type or pattern. In those days a type was made by a blow or force that made an impression on some material. This then became the standard for other similar items which were to be made. That same Greek term is the one from which we get our word *type*.

The Apostle Paul in effect said to Timothy that he was to be a type or pattern of the believer. This is what the Christian leader should be. In so doing, he will establish creditability in our culture at a time when too many seem to be saying, "Do as I say but don't do as I do." At one time the younger generation would accept such a statement, at least superficially. That day is past. Today's generation needs not only exhortation but also exemplification. They observe carefully what the leader does in order to determine for themselves whether he is credible.

A number of graduates of Christian colleges and Bible institutes are not living for God today. Certainly the responsibility lies with them, but part of the reason some of them became disillusioned with Christianity was that they saw in the lives of Christian leaders a contradiction between affirmation and action. That is one reason it is important to understand what is involved in being a type or pattern of the believer.

First of all, consider the use of the term in 1 Thessalonians 1:7, where the Apostle Paul describes the Thessalonian

Christians: "So that ye were ensamples [a type or pattern] to all that believe in Macedonia and Achaia. For from you sounded out the word of the Lord not only in Macedonia and Achaia, but also in every place your faith toward God is spread abroad; so that we need not speak anything. For they themselves shew of us what manner of entering in we had unto you, and how ye turned to God from idols to serve the living and true God; and to wait for his Son from heaven, whom he raised from the dead, even Jesus, which delivered us from the wrath to come." This is a description of a true conversion. Without question, the Christian leader ought to manifest in his life the reality of this kind of conversion.

Such conversion bears three major characteristics. It involves a past action which was determinative, a present state which ought to be normative for the Christian, and a perspective which ought to be regulative of our actions and attitudes.

The past action was turning to God from idols. The reason why we find a great difference between the number of those who make a profession in evangelistic campaigns and the number of those who actually continue on as faithful believers, is that some professed conversions do not involve genuine repentance or turning to God from idols.

Too often the gospel is understood as not requiring an abandonment of one's own supposed righteousness to seek God's forgiveness. Instead it is considered a bargaining agreement akin to that between labor and management. Some come to God and say in effect that they have resources, capabilities, and reputation, and ask what he has to offer in a collective bargaining contract. Sometimes when people talk about having an exciting encounter with a dynamic personality this seems to be what they have in mind. It is existential —a matter of relationship, but not necessarily a matter of abandoning every other allegiance in favor of our Lord Jesus Christ.

Perhaps one reason why coldness and barrenness may enter

the life of a professing Christian is that he or she has a divided allegiance. In a superficial acceptance of Christ there are still other commitments. Consequently, the individual, as described by the Apostle James, is "a double minded man . . . unstable in all his ways."

We must deliberately and consciously say something akin to the words of Toplady's hymn:

> *Nothing in my hand I bring,*
> *Simply to Thy cross I cling;*
> *Naked, come to Thee for dress,*
> *Helpless, look to Thee for grace;*
> *Foul, I to the fountain fly,*
> *Wash me, Savior, or I die!*

This sense of need, this recognition of the utter inadequacy of any other remedy, is essential to repentance. Even those who have come to Christ as children in a very simple and uncomplicated way should have recognized the uniqueness of the Lord Jesus as a personal Savior.

When our Savior set forth the conditions of discipleship, he took this basic element of conversion as a working principle. His statement was, "If any man come to me, and hate not his father, and mother, and wife, and children, and brethren, and sisters, yea, and his own life also, he cannot be my disciple." In effect he was saying, "You have to turn to me from idols, whether these idols be of wood or stone, or whether they be parents, wife, or children, or the worship of one's self."

The second characteristic of conversion is "to serve the true and living God." This makes clear that in conversion we are vitally related to One who is alive and is a God of integrity. A study of the pagan religions discloses just how capricious their deities are. That is why those who worship such deities manifest anxiety. They can never be sure they have done all they should. They fear that their god may change the rules or find some detail they have overlooked. It is not so with God.

He is not only alive so that we may relate to him personally, but he is also true, so that we may relate to him in integrity. He is, as it were, a gentleman who keeps his word, for he is the living and the true God. If a conversion does not produce the ongoing evidence of serving the living and true God, such conversion cannot be real.

Finally, conversion means that we are "to wait for God's Son from heaven." This is the perspective that lifts us beyond those things that could crush us in the pressures of our life today. Many of us know from experience that the enemy can exploit the increasing acceleration of activity in our time to preoccupy us with the immediate present. Then we lose the perspective of waiting for God's Son from heaven.

A surprising number of people cannot endure either silence or reflection about things that matter. Indeed, they are afraid of being caught engaging in quiet reflection. You have seen many young people walking down the street with transistor radios blaring. They seem dependent upon continuous sound. Similarly, the first thing some adults do when they enter the house is to turn on the radio or TV so that they can have sound or sound-plus-picture. I wonder whether they too are afraid of silence or of reflective thinking. Apparently, they don't want to think about the past or the future.

In New England I once had an experience which I shall long remember. I was asked to preach at the 200th anniversary of a church in Westminster, Massachusetts. The members of that church did their best to recreate the conditions of the past. They sang using a tuning fork and having each line of the hymns called out before it was sung. People wore the dress of many decades ago. As the preacher, I wore a top hat, a cut-away coat, and a shirt with a wing collar.

They had arranged that I should come into town in a horse and buggy rather than in an automobile. So I went out to the edge of town, climbed into the buggy, and started for town. On the way I became aware of something I should have known all along. As the horse found his way into the town, I had time

43

to observe the trees and the flowers and really to enjoy the countryside. How different from driving a car and having to watch for oncoming traffic and for obstacles in the road. In the buggy I found time for perspective.

The Christian needs opportunity to contemplate the future, and not just in a casual way. The Apostle Paul makes that point clear by using language that every parent will understand. He says we are to wait expectantly for God's Son from heaven. Parents can remember the evenings when they waited up for the children to come home—and were grateful when they heard the door open. The Apostle Paul has identified such an expectant attitude as one of the evidences of our conversion. We are to be believers who have made a radical break with all past allegiances in favor of a continuing singular commitment to Jesus Christ, but who are also now waiting with eager anticipation the return of God's Son from heaven.

Even though we may die before he returns, the perspective is still there. The Christian leader must manifest this perspective and not fall prey to the curse of overactivity that denies us the privilege of thinking about things ultimate as well as things immediate.

These are the characteristics of a credible and a comprehensive conversion, one that you and I are called to exemplify as Christian leaders.

The second reference to the term *example* is found in 2 Thessalonians 3, beginning at verse 7: "For ye yourselves know how ye ought to follow us: for we behaved not ourselves disorderly among you; neither did we eat any man's bread for nothing; but wrought with labor and travail night and day, that we might not be chargeable to any of you; not because we have not power [or the authority or the privilege], but to make ourselves an example unto you to follow us. For even when we were with you, this we commanded you, that if any would not work, neither should he eat. For we hear there are some who walk among you disorderly, working not at all, but are busybodies. Now them that are such we command and exhort by our Lord Jesus Christ, that with quietness they work, and eat their own bread. But ye brethren, be not weary in well doing."

This passage teaches us that we are to be examples of the believer in the responsible way in which we manage our affairs and assume responsibility for the meeting of our temporal needs. Unfortunately, a parasitic attitude sometimes rears its head even in the Christian community. A person with such an attitude expects others to do what he should do for himself. This can become a problem to Christian leaders. Leaders are often the recipients of the goodness and the care and attention of others—especially if they are eloquent or have a dynamic personality. People just naturally put such leaders in a special category.

I recall being in an elevator in the Mayo Clinic with Billy Graham. A lady got on the elevator, looked at him, and asked, "Are you Billy Graham?" When he said, "Yes, ma'am," she touched him and then said, "Now I know I am going to get better because I touched you." In response Dr. Graham said, "Ma'am, I don't have any power. You should trust the Lord. He is able to help you."

Leaders with charm and a charismatic personality frequently receive favors from others. It is not always easy in such circumstances to do what this passage says. Certainly, Paul as an apostle could have expected the Thessalonians to take care of his needs. But to be an example to them, he took care of those needs himself, to give them an illustration of self-reliance and of consistency. Thus they could see in him a model—a person who did his work just as they were expected to do theirs.

By personality and temperament some find it hard to accept favors. When we are commended for having done a good job, we are tempted to respond by depreciating our performance. The problem is that after a while it sounds as though we are playing games and encouraging the other person to make an even stronger case in our favor until we finally are justified in agreeing. Or we may find it hard to accept deserved praise, or to receive a gift without feeling that we must do something in return for our benefactor. What's needed is a proper balance that accepts deserved praise gracefully but does not presume upon the kindness and consideration of others. This means that we will be scrupulous in the way we take care of our personal affairs. Thus we provide an example of self-reliance and dependability.

While serving a church in the city of Brockton, Massachusetts, I opened an account at a men's clothing store. The salesman told me they were glad to have me as a customer, but then remarked that some of the local ministers, when called to another parish, left without paying their bills. Thus, while the store was willing to open an account for a clergyman, they were not enthusiastic about it.

I received a somewhat similar reaction from a Christian businessman in the greater Chicago area. He said that whenever he did business with a man who carried a New Testament in his vest pocket he became cautious because he had had unfortunate experiences with such people.

It has grieved me to hear these things about some of my fellow ministers and about some Christians who are in business. Apparently they thought that those with whom they did business, particularly if they too were Christians, should give them something for nothing. They felt it was quite legitimate to make a sharp deal or to leave unpaid bills, assuming that the other man could afford to make up the loss. But the Apostle Paul's exhortation to work and to eat our own bread applies to such things as paying our accounts and seeing to it that our business dealings are scrupulously honest.

Exemplary behavior in these matters will convey both to our fellow Christians and to non-Christians what it means to be a believer. It will also help to offset the attitude of some non-Christians who say they do not want to become Christians because they cannot trust Christians as much as they can trust some of their non-Christian friends. Unfortunately, there is just enough truth in this statement to be painful. And the problem is all the more serious if the inconsistency occurs in the life of a Christian leader.

I remember being asked by a prominent Christian to give an address. I drove quite a distance to speak to the group. When I left he shook my hand and said, "You'll be hearing from me." To this day I have heard nothing from him, not even a word of explanation that there were no funds for travel expenses or an honorarium. Christian leaders must recognize that others notice such behavior and are disillusioned by it. On the other hand, when we are honest in business and honor our obligations, our example confirms our message.

It is helpful here to recognize the scope of the third commandment's meaning. The commandment says, "Thou shalt not take the name of the Lord thy God in vain." This does not refer just to profanity when the name of God is used in swearing. It also means that we do not take the name of God in a vain way in our dealings with other people. It is as if we had the trademark of God's name on us and we therefore must be sure the trademark reflects the authenticity of the name we bear.

The third usage of the word *example* is in Philippians 3:17. There the Apostle Paul says, "Brethren, be followers together of me, and mark them who walk even as you have us for an example. (For many walk, of whom I have told you often, and now tell you even weeping, that they are the enemies of the cross of Christ: Whose end is destruction, whose God is their appetite, and whose glory is in their shame, who mind earthly things.) For our citizenship is in heaven . . . "

Karl Marx said that his philosophy of dialectical materialism was calculated to turn that of the philosopher Hegel upside down. While Hegel spoke of an over-arching idea, Marx proposed to turn it upside down so that dialectical materialism could prevail.

Some in our American culture today are dedicated to turning human beings upside down by making the cerebral subordinate to the visceral or to the genital. Often what they describe as avant-garde or bold or daring or creative is simply turning the human being upside down. That's what the Apostle Paul is saying here: The belly is elevated as an object of worship.

Christian leaders face almost incredible assaults along these lines. Their temptations are not only sexual but also of the whole range of self-indulgence. When Scripture speaks of their god being their appetite, this means that whether it is things, or creature comforts, or sex, or fame, or power, there is an insatiable appetite for self-gratification. To control the self-gratification urge, the Christian leader must learn to practice mental self-discipline. A failure to do this is the reason why some in Christian leadership have made shipwreck of their lives.

Some time ago a gifted preacher came to visit us and we went out with mutual friends for a meal. Throughout the evening this man dominated the conversation, orienting it toward himself. His preoccupation with his own interests became painfully obvious. Not too many months later, he left the ministry because in his insatiable desire for self-gratification he had engaged in immorality.

He had permitted his appetites to become his god. They dominated him. He had allowed himself to be turned upside down. The spiritual was subordinated to the physical and emotional. Nor is his case unique. Christian leaders are subject to this kind of temptation to an exceptional degree because there are always those who are prepared to indulge the leader in one way or another if he will allow it.

Some time ago, I read about a man who sought to cultivate more self-discipline by eating only potatoes for thirty days. Another man, learning of this, decided that he would do the same with peanut butter and buttermilk for the same period of time. From personal experience I know that a test of this kind can be beneficial.

After graduating from Wheaton College, I went to Clark University in Massachusetts for graduate study. I had been awarded a scholarship with a stipend that allowed for luncheon and dinner six days a week. Since I felt the need for breakfast each day as well, I used the small amount of money I had to buy each week a box of shredded wheat, a can of condensed milk, and a pound of brown sugar. Every morning I would put two shredded wheat biscuits in a bowl, pour some condensed milk on them, add water, and top that with a liberal portion of brown sugar. For two semesters I had the same breakfast each morning: shredded wheat, brown sugar, condensed milk. I confess that it was some years before I could enjoy shredded wheat again, but the discipline dictated by my lack of funds was good for me. I believe I appreciated my education more. And later I certainly appreciated the more varied breakfasts I was able to afford.

Such discipline, however, involves only physical or external matters. More critical is the self-discipline of the mind, because it is there that the struggle first takes place. Our football coach tells his players, "You give up first in your mind; then your body quits." Similarly, we give up first in our minds, and then we actually engage in self-indulgence, whether for material things or fame or reputation or sex or whatever we think we must have. Discipline of the mind is essential to disciplined behavior. The Christian leader of integrity is one who so disciplines his mind that he is not overcome by temptation or adversely affected by externals.

This was impressed upon me by a man who for some years was chairman of the board of Gordon Collge, Mr. William Sheppard. When I was leaving Gordon to come to Wheaton, the president asked me to preach the baccalaureate sermon, something which he usually did himself. I considered it a great honor and I prepared diligently for the occasion. After the service, people came to me to offer their congratulations. Then Mr. Sheppard came to me and said, "Thank you for a good message. Now let me share something with you. Praise is like horse liniment."

I really did not understand what he meant. I asked him to

explain. With a twinkle in his eye he said, "It's useful as long as it isn't taken internally." It was a needful bit of homely wisdom that I have found very helpful.

Some of the most godly people I know are the ones who are the most sensitive to the presence of sin in their own lives. The closer they are to the Lord, the more they recognize things that need to be corrected. It is encouraging also to know that in our Christian walk God does not give up on us (unless we force the matter), but encourages us to grow and to become aware of anything in our lives that needs to be brought more under his jurisdiction.

An effective Christian leader then will recognize that what is in his mind will be reflected in his behavior pattern. That's why it's essential to cultivate a personal holiness that will express itself in day-to-day living and will reflect discipline rather than simply self-gratification.

The final reference to *example* that we shall consider is in Titus 2, beginning with verse 6: "Young men likewise exhort to be sober minded. In all things shewing thyself a pattern of good works: in doctrine shewing uncorruptness, gravity, sincerity, sound speech, that cannot be condemned; that he that is of the contrary part may be ashamed, having no evil thing to say of you."

This passage seems to summarize the ministry of example, for it refers to our philsophy of life, the way we have determined we are going to live, and the convictions that we think are essential. The Apostle Paul sums this up as "uncorruptness, gravity, sincerity, sound speech that cannot be condemned."

Unfortunately, much of what passes for Christian faith tends to be superficial and naive. This should not be. Instead, the believer ought to be willing to face the major issues of life and diligently search the Holy Scriptures in order to come to a settled conviction about these matters. Then he will express his philosophy of life in a practical way that is honoring to the Lord and edifying to others.

Furthermore, the ministry of example is not limited to individuals. From both 1 Thessalonians 1 and 1 Corinthians 10 we see that there is also a corporate example. God ordained that Israel would be an example to the nations. To illustrate his dealings with a covenant people, he selected one small segment of mankind. What he did was akin to our practice of testing to see whether a reservoir of water is pure. We need not drain the whole reservoir and test all the millions of gallons of water in it. Instead we take samples, and if the samples prove pure we consider the whole reservoir pure.

Thus the Apostle Paul emphasized that the things that happened to Israel were to be an example to us, upon whom the ends of the ages are come. We should keep this in mind in our involvement with our churches and other Christian organizations. Each Christian body is a corporate example for the world and all the heavenly host to observe. Leaders of the churches and other groups have a major responsibility to insure that the corporate witness is vital and effective.

CHAPTER FIVE
WORDS
Matthew 12:33-37

LET US CONSIDER WHAT it means to be an example of the believer in word. A biblical statement about the importance of words is found in Matthew 12:33-37. Here our Savior says, "Either make the tree good, and its fruit good; or else make the tree corrupt, and its fruit corrupt, for the tree is known by its fruit. O generation of vipers, how can ye, being evil, speak good things? for out of the abundance of the heart the mouth speaketh. A good man out of the good treasure of the heart bringeth forth good things; and an evil man out of the evil treasure bringeth forth evil things. But I say unto you, That every idle word that men shall speak, they shall give account of it in the day of judgment. For by thy words thou shalt be justified, and by thy words thou shalt be condemned."

In 1932 a book entitled *Re-thinking Missions* made its first appearance. This volume was a layman's inquiry into the missionary enterprise after approximately one hundred years of American involvement. Its editor was William Ernest Hocking, a philosopher from Harvard University. In this volume the writers sought to evaluate the missionary enterprise and to make some suggestions for the future. Their viewpoint was not theologically orthodox. One portion declared that ministry to the secular needs of men in the spirit of Christ is evangelism in the right use of the word.

I presume that what Dr. Hocking and his associates meant by this was that a verbalized witness for Jesus Christ was no longer adequate; instead, meaningful service was to be preferred. Kindness and concern expressed in service would attract people to Jesus Christ.

Evangelicals agree that Scripture specifies we are to engage in acts of mercy, of helpfulness and of concern. But this does not take the place of statements which declare the biblical message of the gospel.

This issue came up in a discussion at a conference I attended some years ago while my wife and I were associated with Gordon College in Massachusetts. A group of us were meeting on Gibson Island, off the east coast of the United States, to discuss some political matters. A professor of a nearby college, who met with us, observed that Jesus never talked about his faith but simply went about doing good. In response I asked how long it had been since he had read the New Testament. He admitted that he had not done so recently. I then observed that if he would consult the New Testament, as the most credible record about Jesus, he would find that Jesus not only did good deeds, but also spoke at length to the people to declare his message to them.

Words are important. Their significance is evident both in the nature of God and in the nature of man. And their significance is evident particularly in the Scripture's emphasis upon the fact that God holds us accountable for what we say.

First consider whether words are significant as far as the nature of God is concerned. Some might say that the metaphysical union of Father, Son, and Holy Spirit does not require verbalized communication. In their integral relationship, the members of the Trinity might seem not to need to speak to one another. But in Genesis 1:26 we have an indication that conversation does take place within the Trinity. To be sure, this statement is in a portion of Scripture that some consider symbolic or mythical. Dr. Francis Schaeffer has written a book entitled *Genesis in Space and Time*, that speaks to the question of whether the first eleven chapters of Genesis describe specific events in space and time, or whether they are mythological. Some who take a different view of these early chapters of Genesis see them as symbolic stories conveying truth somewhat in the way that Aesop's Fables do. Personally, I believe these chapters describe specific happenings in space and time and that what is mentioned in Genesis 1:26 actually occurred.

Notice the statement: "And God said, Let us make man in our image, after our likeness; and let them have dominion over the fish of the sea, and over the fowl of the air . . ." Scripture here portrays the Trinity engaged in conversation. Similarly, in Genesis 11:7 the verse reads, "Let us go down, and there confound their language . . ." We may infer that the Father was speaking to the Son and to the Holy Spirit, for while each of the persons in the Trinity is equal, there is a sense in which, as far as sovereign oversight is concerned, God the Father—not the Son or the Holy Spirit—exercises this prerogative. Thus, it is probable that the Father is speaking in these references, using words in communicating with the Son and the Holy Spirit.

We should also recognize that when our Lord Jesus Christ came to earth, he was called The Word. This term connotes reasoned discourse. While he was called the Messiah and while he manifested the Father in his Person, it is significant that he was also called The Logos, the reasoned discourse. This suggests something about the nature of God's revelation which should be kept in mind. Jesus Christ personified what God wanted to be understood by reasoned discourse. Thus, this understanding was not simply conveyed through dramatic acts but through statements which our Savior made. By his actions he confirmed that it was by reasoned discourse that God has chosen to reveal himself to man.

Similarly, the Holy Spirit ministers explicitly through words. The Holy Spirit's ministry of words is essential to the doctrine of the verbal inspiration of Scripture. A key statement about this appears in 1 Corinthians 2. Here the Apostle Paul explains that men can understand one another because they have the same spirit but in their sinful state cannot understand the things of God because they do not have the Holy Spirit. Paul says, "The natural man receiveth not the things of the Spirit of God: for they are foolishness unto him: neither can he know them, because they are spiritually discerned." In this same context (verse 13) the apostle says, "Which things also we speak, not in the words which man's wisdom teacheth, but which the Holy Spirit teacheth; comparing spiritual things with spiritual."

Evangelicals believe that the Holy Spirit guided the writers of Scripture in the choice of their words. The process was not dictation. Rather it was the providential guidance of the Spirit of God. Within the limits of each writer's personality and style, the Spirit moved upon the Scripture writers to choose the words which were essential for the transmission of God's truth. Furthermore, the Holy Spirit enables earnest readers to understand these words and thus to grasp God's truth verbally conveyed.

Thus, God reveals truth not only in the phenomena of nature and in what he has written upon the heart of man, but also in propositional truth. Hence, this revelation is not simply inferred from actions, feelings, encounters, or relationships. It is articulated verbally.

This view of revelation distinguishes evangelicals from others in the religious community who argue that meaning can be gained only by experience or by encounter. Words are therefore essential not only to a full understanding of God's truth but also to an adequate response to that truth. For example, words were a vital part of our coming to God in Jesus Christ. Romans 10:9 specifies that we are to confess the Lord Jesus Christ with our mouths besides believing in our hearts in order to be saved. While with the heart a person believes unto righteousness, it is with the mouth that he makes confession unto salvation. We do this because we have in our minds grasped the essentials of the gospel. Further, Scripture teaches us (1 John 4:2) that we make this confession because of the ministry of the Holy Spirit; it is he who enables us to confess Jesus Christ as Lord.

The Spirit of God, therefore, not only inspired the writers of Holy Scripture to write down propositional truth so that we might have it in words, but also convinced us that we are sinners in need of a Savior—and enabled us to confess Jesus as Lord.

After we have thus received him, we can claim the great promise of Acts 1:8: "Ye shall receive power, after that the Holy Spirit is come upon you: and ye shall be witnesses unto me . . ." The Spirit of God overcomes to a significant degree the problem of communication that became so severe at the Tower of Babel. In fact, it is fascinating to contrast the confusion of the Tower of Babel with the coherence made possible by the Holy Spirit at Pentecost and afterward. Because of his work we may both understand and communicate the truth of the Word of God.

From the experiences of daily life we know that we can hear without understanding. Parents say in exasperation, "How many times do I have to tell you?" because the children have said, "Yes, Mother," or "Yes, Daddy," without really grasping what was said. To be sure, this is due in part to inattention, but not entirely so.

Some years ago I taught a course in Asian history. In that course I dealt, among other things, with one of the Asian religions, Taoism. The opening statement of the Tao Te Ching can be translated this way: "The way that can be understood is not the real way."

My students, being Western in their thought patterns, would frequently conclude that the statement did not make sense. After all, if the way that can be understood is not the real way, how would it ever be possible to know the real way?

I suggested that possibly Laotzu by common grace had gained some idea of the nature and being of God. I then observed that the line might be translated: "The God that can be fully understood is not really God." At that point they began to recognize the importance of the statement. They saw that if they could fully describe and classify God, he would no longer be infinite but finite.

In a far more sublime way, when you and I bear witness to Jesus Christ as Savior and Lord, as the Spirit of God enables us to do, our witness is understood through the ministry of that same Holy Spirit. In this way our words communicate God's truth. This gives a deep significance to words.

In our day many seem to believe that words do not really mean anything. Listeners to some public figures have gained the impression that what public speakers say is not really what is to be believed but is simply something for the record.

We should not conclude from this that the public servants of today are necessarily more untruthful than those of previous generations. Our awareness of their inconsistency may simply arise from the fact that today we have what the previous generations did not have—instant replay. Years ago a public figure could deny saying something. It might have taken weeks for the word to get to the local community, or perhaps nobody had recorded it, or those who wrote it down might have been mistaken. But today, a technician just needs to press a button and in living color the official repeats exactly what he might otherwise be tempted to deny he had said.

Incidentally, this is the way it will be in eternity. All along, God has had instant replay, and he will hold us accountable for what we have said. His reason for doing so is that there is an integral relationship between what we say and what we are. This fact is difficult for some to accept. They may insist that they were joking or that they really did not mean what they said. But Scripture suggests the opposite.

Notice the statement in Matthew 12:33, where the Lord uses an illustration of a tree and its fruit: "The tree is known by its fruit." We do not come to one kind of tree and expect to find another kind of fruit on it. The Apostle James says the same thing about a fountain of water. We do not expect a fountain to bring forth both salt water and fresh water at the same time. Scripture shows that our speech reflects the way we really are inside.

The next verse explains why. "Out of the abundance of the heart the mouth speaketh." Essential to a proper understanding of this statement is a grasp of the meaning of the term heart. An excellent summary is found in Romans 10. Verse 1 reads: "Brethren, my heart's desire and prayer to God for Israel is, that they might be saved." This makes plain that the heart has desires or emotions.

Verse 6 says: "But the righteousness which is of faith speaketh on this wise, Say not in thine heart, Who shall ascend into heaven? (that is, to bring Christ down from above:) Or, Who shall descend into the deep? (that is, to bring up Christ again from the dead)." This indicates that the heart is capable of speculative thought. In his heart the individual is reasoning with himself. Probably everyone has had the experience of arguing with himself or talking to himself.

Then in the tenth verse the apostle says, "For with the heart man believeth unto righteousness . . ." Obviously, this is an act of the will. Belief is a commitment. When we say that we believe something, and we mean it, we have by an act of the will made a commitment.

If we define a human being as one possessing rationality, emotion, and will, then the term *heart* as used in Holy Scripture refers to the essential makeup of the individual, that which characterizes us as persons. Therefore, when the Savior says, "out of the abundance of the heart the mouth speaketh," he is saying that it is out of the total personality that the mouth speaks.

Consider also the matter of the abundance of the heart. An illustration of the concept of abundance is found in Mark 8. This passage describes the feeding of the four thousand. Verse 8 says: "So they did eat, and were filled: and they took up of the broken pieces that were left [the abundance that was remaining] seven baskets." In other words, abundance is an overflow or a surplus. As far as the abundance of the heart is concerned, it is an outpouring that discloses the real person.

For a number of years I have been involved in hiring faculty members. Early in my experience I would sometimes recommend a candidate only on the basis of correspondence. If the candidate came to campus, I thought it was adequate if he would spend an hour or two, and then leave. In the process I learned two important facts. The first was that written references are not very reliable. In fact, they sometimes leave out what is vital.

I recall recommending a candidate for appointment only to find out after he had been on campus for a few months that he was emotionally disturbed. When I checked his references to see if there was any intimation of this problem, I found none. After we got in touch with those who had completed references on him, however, they acknowledged they knew he had this problem. When asked why they failed to mention it, they said they did not want to hurt his career. We now ask for references by telephone and assess not only the statements we get but also any evidences of enthusiasm or reluctance that would seem to justify more exploration.

The other fact I learned was that a brief interview is not very satisfactory. Candidates usually appeared sartorially perfect and with their responses carefully rehearsed. Sometimes it seemed as if they had read a book on interviews and were following a recommended pattern of behavior. Having read some of the same books, I found their responses amusing. But I was not getting accurate impressions of the candidates. It was all too formal and structured to permit them to be themselves. So I asked that each candidate be with us for several hours, preferably overnight. After some time had passed, the candidate could relax and talk freely. Then I saw more of the real person. From uninhibited conversation I gained an insight previously hidden.

By personal observation and experience we know that our

conversation will turn to what really interests us. When we are relaxed with family or intimate friends, our speech discloses our real value structure rather than that which we may evidence only on special occasions.

We have a son who is now in medical school. When he was younger, he had an absorbing interest in major league baseball. In our times together as a family it would not take long before he would mention who was the most valuable player of the league or who had the highest batting average. We had no difficulty concluding that baseball was of primary interest to him.

Adults have the same tendency. When they are relaxed, they talk about what interests them. Aboard the aircraft carrier USS *Independence,* I ate in the wardroom with the pilots—officers who had been flying for years. As I listened to their conversation, they talked about airplanes and little else. They discussed performance, fuel consumption, landings, and formations. No one needed to tell me what their primary interest was; it was airplanes.

The fact that our uninhibited speech reveals what we really are should be a cause for realistic self-examination and for appropriate corrective action. We cannot presume that being in a position of Christian leadership guarantees a predictable speech pattern. On occasion I have been disillusioned to hear Christian leaders relate anecdotes of questionable taste. I have also heard some leaders use humor that is at the expense of another. When I observe an individual who is habitually depreciating others and telling jokes at their expense, I ask myself what it is that motivates such talk. Often such hostility against others springs from an inadequacy or an insecurity.

My wife and I have friends in Chicago who came to Christ as adults. When we go to their home to visit, they may occasionally talk about their non-Christian past, but generally they are eager to share just how wonderful the Lord is to them today—or how a particular passage of Scripture is blessing their lives. On occasion I am moved to tears as they talk about their love for the Lord Jesus. Surely I do not need to ask what the abundance of their hearts is. It is the Lord Jesus, and his holy Word.

What has been said about the abundance of the heart relates directly to what follows in the text: "But I say unto you, That every idle word that men shall speak, they shall give account thereof in the day of judgment. For by thy words thou shalt be justified, and by thy words thou shalt be condemned" (Matthew 12:36, 37). The careless or idle word is the un-inhibited word, the word that accurately represents the inner condition. The Lord holds us accountable for these because such speech is a reflection of our inner being, the way we really are.

It follows then that a change of speech begins from within. Unless we focus our attention on the things that are "true, honest, just, pure, lovely and of good report," these will be displaced by other things. Nature abhors a vacuum. So does the individual. If we do not think upon the things Scripture enumerates, other things will surely enter in. And then, just as surely, a careless word will reflect the way we really are.

I became painfully aware of this while serving in the Navy. Once while we were in a combat zone, we received orders to have the anti-aircraft battery manned. However, the officer of the deck needed some men to handle lines. So a young Ensign took a gun crew from their stations to handle the lines. These men were part of my division. I soon found out that they had left the anti-aircraft battery unmanned because of this Ensign's action. I can remember yet calling the Ensign to the anti-aircraft battery control station and in front of some of the crew describing him as a certain kind of fool.

The moment I did so I realized that I had cursed him. I went back to my room terribly discouraged with myself. Aboard ship I had been conducting a Bible class, and in other ways had endeavored to witness for the Lord. How could I, a Christian, have acted this way? Then I realized what I had been doing. Day by day I had listened to profanity all around me. After a while when I became terribly provoked, I would think profanity but would not say it. Then when I became very angry I swore because my inhibitions were gone. What had been in my mind inevitably came out in words.

To avoid such an outburst requires constant attention and mental discipline. Even now I must be on my guard. Recently a dear friend came to say hello. At that time I was under terrible pressure. Though I responded to his greeting I am sure I was saying in effect, "What do you mean interrupting my schedule when I don't have any time to see you?" I felt obliged to write to that colleague and apologize. It was obvious I had not dealt with the problem within. I had failed to say to myself that I was getting too frustrated and annoyed and tense. I needed to ask the Lord for grace and strength. Too often we destroy in an instant what took months or years to develop, because of the condition of our hearts that finds expression in our mouths.

Often the solution to this problem lies in our ability to say no. It may be necessary to resign from some boards and committees because of having become encumbered with too many responsibilities. I do not believe it is the will of God for people to be stretched beyond their capacity until they are unable to cope with their responsibilities.

As Christian leaders, therefore, let us take time to cultivate our inner being through prayer and meditation upon God's Word—and then be sensible about our schedules and responsibilities. In so doing we shall have speech that is always "with grace, seasoned with salt." And by our words we will be justified.

CHAPTER SIX
MANNER OF LIFE
Ephesians 4:17-24

THE SECOND FACTOR in being an example of the believer has to do with our manner of life—the way in which we normally live. Several portions of Scripture provide insights into this matter. Consider, first, Ephesians 4:17-24:

"This I say therefore, and testify in the Lord, that ye henceforth walk not as other Gentiles walk, in the vanity of their mind, having the understanding darkened, being alienated from the life of God through the ignorance that is in them, because of the blindness of their heart: who being past feeling have given themselves over unto lasciviousness, to work all uncleanness with greediness. But ye have not so learned Christ; if so be that ye have heard him, and have been taught by him, as the truth is in Jesus: that ye put off concerning the former conversation the old man, which is corrupt according to the deceitful lusts; and be renewed in the spirit of your mind; and that ye put on the new man, which after God is created in righteousness and true holiness."

After saying this, Paul specifies what it means: putting off falsehood and speaking truthfully, being angry without sinning, not giving the devil a foothold, no longer stealing, not letting any unwholesome talk come out of your mouth, not grieving the Holy Spirit, getting rid of bitterness, rage, brawling, and slander, along with every form of malice. These are the particulars.

Two passages of Galatians are pertinent here. "Be not deceived; God is not mocked: for whatsoever a man soweth, that shall he also reap. For he that soweth to his flesh shall of the flesh reap corruption; but he that soweth to the Spirit shall of the Spirit reap life everlasting. And let us not be weary in well doing: for in due season we shall reap, if we faint not" (Galatians 6:7-9).

Related to this passage is the following: "This I say then, Walk in the Spirit, and ye shall not fulfill the lust of the flesh. For the flesh lusteth against the Spirit, and the Spirit against the flesh; and these are contrary the one to the other: so that ye cannot do the things that ye would. But if ye be led of the Spirit, ye are not under the law. Now the works of the flesh are manifest, which are these: adultery, fornication, uncleanness, lasciviousness, idolatry, witchcraft, hatred, variance, emulations, wrath, strife, seditions, heresies, envyings, murders, drunkenness, revellings, and such like: of the which I tell you before, as I have also told you in times past, that they which do such things shall not inherit the kingdom of God" (Galatians 5:16-21).

In our pattern of living we face the need for making a basic choice, something that non-Christians do not really face because they are only in the flesh. Scripture says that those who have not become spiritually alive cannot please God because their minds are darkened and their sensitivities dulled. Thus they are unable to respond because sin does not give them an option.

On the other hand, when one becomes a Christian, he is at that point given an option. He needs to make a choice. If this were not so, the exhortations in the Bible would be meaningless. That's why I have a problem with those who claim to have arrived at the point of sinless perfection. In my judgment, the Christian, as long as he is in this scene, will need to choose between the flesh and the Spirit. As he grows in grace and knowledge, he will progressively align his life with the teachings of Scripture. But we are on dangerous ground if we equate positional sanctification with what is called practical or progressive sanctification, being set apart for God.

When we become Christians, we are redeemed. The words that Scripture uses for redemption are the same words that refer to the purchase of slaves in a slave market: taking slaves out of the market entirely, and then setting them free. Scripture repeatedly makes the point that once this happens, then it is the responsibility of the Christian increasingly to make true in actuality what is true of him positionally.

I learned the difference between position and practice when I entered the Navy during World War Two. I was what was called in those days a ninety-day wonder. Four years of college and ninety days of naval training—then we were positionally naval officers. Unfortunately, a one-day cruise down the Hudson River on a patrol craft was all the sea duty we had experienced.

After commissioning I reported aboard the USS *Wichita* on December 3, 1942. On the train from New York to Norfolk a sailor who had frequented the bar on the train saluted me and asked my judgment on a matter. I was impressed at how much that single gold stripe meant. But once aboard ship it was an entirely different situation. Then the theory had to be put into practice. My division officer and his men looked condescendingly at me while I tried to remember what I had read about the main features of a combatant ship. I was really struggling and they all knew it.

The next three months were extraordinarily painful for me because I was seasick and homesick. And yet I had to make good in practice what I was in position. After all, I was a commissioned officer in the United States Navy!

That's the issue that faces the Christian. We are to make good in practice what we are in position, by sowing to the Spirit rather than the flesh. But there is a tough question implicit in Galatians 6. Is it possible for a Christian to have a manner of life antithetical to that which a believer's manner of life is supposed to be? I believe that it is possible. When the Apostle Paul enumerated the works of the flesh in Galatians 5, he was indicating the possibility of even a Christian doing such things. Otherwise, what was the point of his saying to the Galatian Christians, "Live by the Spirit and you will not gratify the desires of your sinful nature"? Paul also emphasized that the Spirit and the sinful nature are in conflict with each other so that we do not do what we want to do.

This can be interpreted in two different ways. The first of these is that we cannot do the things we want to do spiritually, because our flesh opposes such doing. The other view, which I prefer, is that because of the indwelling presence of the Holy Spirit, we do not do the things that we might want to do naturally, because he is there to restrain and to control.

In the event any may feel that the practices of the flesh could not be present in the Christian church, consider 1 Corinthians 5:1, 2. From the salutation in chapter one we know that the man mentioned here had confessed Jesus Christ as Savior and had been admitted to the fellowship of the church. Yet he had engaged in a sexual sin that the apostle said was not even practiced among the pagans.

In response to Paul's rebuke, the Corinthian church disciplined that member. Thankfully, that was not all that happened. We know this from 2 Corinthians 2:3-11, where Paul urged acceptance and restoration. I believe the individual to whom the Apostle Paul referred was the same man mentioned in 1 Corinthians 5. The point is that the Christian may choose to go the way of the flesh. The wonderful thing is that he does not *need* to adopt such a manner of life, because he can elect to live under the power and guidance of the Holy Spirit and thus be controlled by the Spirit rather than by the flesh.

To do this effectively the Christian must take some decisive action. This is described in the sixth chapter of Romans: "For in that he [that is, Christ] died, he died unto sin once: but in that he liveth, he liveth unto God. Likewise reckon ye also yourselves to be dead indeed unto sin, but alive unto God through Jesus Christ our Lord. Let not sin therefore reign in your mortal body, that you should obey it in the lusts thereof. Neither yield ye your members as instruments of unrighteousness unto sin: but yield yourselves unto God, as those that are alive from the dead, and your members as instruments of righteousness unto God" (Romans 6:10-13).

What is meant by reckoning? An illustration from navigation may help explain this. When a ship is at sea, the navigator goes up on the bridge to take his evening star sights. Then when he has plotted these on his chart, he gets a "fix"—if he has done his work right. This means that all the lines come together in one place.

After the 8 o'clock position has been calculated, the commanding officer, in his night order book, specifies the various courses and speeds for the night. For example, he may say that between 2000 and 2400 the ship is to steam on course 090 at 16 knots. At 0300 the ship is to change course to 180 and slow to 10 knots and remain at that course and speed until 0800. The navigator plots all that on the chart. Then the officer of the deck, who is in charge of the ship for the period of time he is on watch, gives these orders to the helmsman and to the engine room. These orders are based upon what we used to call "dead reckoning." It took into account the state of the sea, the fouling of the hull, and the direction and velocity of the wind and the current.

By next morning, when the navigator took the morning star sights, if everything worked out according to plan, the ship was at the 0800 position. What had been done? The captain took the information that was in hand, gave orders based upon this information, and the ship was directed accordingly toward a known destination.

The same principle applies to the Christian way of life. The

Word of God tells us Jesus Christ has died and now has been raised in newness of life. Based upon this, we are to reckon—that is, to assume—that we are dead to sin because of our relationship to Jesus Christ. And we are further to assume that because he is now alive, we also are alive in a new situation. Therefore as a result we must not yield our capabilities unto sin, because we have passed from one state of being to another. Furthermore, we must take positive action and not stay in a position of neutrality.

The officer of the deck could not say, "We will stay here until we can see daylight, and then we will go on." Not at all. Likewise the Christian, having determined that he will not yield his capabilities to sin, must take the next step. Scripture makes a very interesting and, I think, significant statement about this that sometimes we may miss. It is this: "Yield yourselves unto God, as those that are alive from the dead, and your members as instruments of righteousness unto God."

Do you know what sometimes happens when we attempt to establish a manner of life pleasing to God? We reverse the sequence of Scripture and yield our *capabilities* to God before we submit *ourselves* to him. The results are predictable. Because we have not yielded ourselves to God, we find the yielding of our capabilities to be spasmodic or incomplete. Since our basic commitment is tentative or absent, the willingness to place our capabilities unreservedly at the disposal of the Lord is subject to the whims of the moment.

Instead, there should be the decisive subordination of ourselves to him. Then we will give our specific gifts to the Lord as a logical product of our commitment. When the Christian leader refuses to yield his abilities as instruments of unrighteousness unto sin, but instead yields himself to God and places his abilities at his disposal, then he is ready to be of constructive usefulness in the fellowship of God's people.

A number of New Testament scholars have suggested that the passage in 1 Corinthians 3 that deals with building upon

Christ as the foundation refers to a group rather than to an individual. In other words, those doing the building are contributing to a body of believers rather than simply to their own personal lives.

The imagery the apostle used is vivid. The constructive contribution is called gold, silver, and precious stones. The strictly self-serving efforts are described as wood, hay, and stubble. The testing agent is fire. The Christian leader who seeks the best interest of the group he serves will be building with gold, silver, and precious stones. But the one who does not do this will see the wood, hay, and stubble of his misguided efforts burned.

I am persuaded that some prominent Christian leaders who did not choose to live under the control of the Holy Spirit but instead indulged their fleshly desires will see what the world might call "a lifetime of success" reduced to ashes.

Part of the reason for their error in judgment is their tendency to quantify their work, whereas God's criterion is quality. In other words, one person might have an enormous structure of wood, hay, and stubble, while someone else would have a very small structure of gold, silver, and precious stones. The carnal man would boast, "Consider my building. Notice its generous dimensions and its prominent location. See how it has become a landmark and a civic attraction for all to see. As for this other structure of gold, silver, and precious stones, is there anything noteworthy about it? It is so small that it is insignificant."

But suppose a fire sweeps through the city that night. The next morning the carnal man stands amid the ashes of his once great edifice, while the spiritual man's building has come through unscathed. His contribution to the corporate body was with materials that survived the test of fire.

For the Christian leader to be able to do this, he must first of all determine that the will of God is primary in his life. Having resolved to glorify God in his body and spirit because by redemption these are God's, he is then liberated to serve God's people wherever he is sent, without regard for status or personal reward.

Some years ago I came to know a winsome young man. He had completed his high school education more on his personality and his athletic prowess than on his academic achievements. When he entered college, however, the system that worked so successfully in high school failed him. His low grades forced him to withdraw from college. The shock of this experience brought him to his senses, however, and at another college he did very well. On the basis of his improved scholastic record he gained readmittance to the college where he had begun his work. In due course he was graduated. Then he successfully finished seminary and entered the ministry.

In time he became pastor of a thriving church. Under his leadership the church grew in numbers and resources. To his associates he was known as a successful pastor. Then one day he announced his resignation. People were bewildered and wondered if he was not being paid enough or if he needed more privileges and benefits. On the contrary, they found he had accepted a call to a much smaller church in a far more obscure location and at a lower salary. His explanation was simple. God had called him, and he was responding to that call.

The fact that the church was smaller and that the salary was less was of no consequence. He had determined that he would do the will of God without regard to perquisites or prominence. As I heard this, I was both refreshed and challenged. Here was an illustration of one who had yielded himself to the Lord and put his abilities at God's disposal. I concluded that his contribution to his congregation would be gold, silver, and precious stones, because he had chosen to give himself to the things of the Spirit rather than to the things of the flesh.

This is what it means for the Christian leader to be an example in manner of life. Such a pattern cannot help but provide to others a tangible illustration of authentic Christian living. That, after all, is essential to the high and holy calling of Christian leadership. But it will involve a consistent obedience to the Scripture's teachings about Christian practice.

As an illustration, consider the teaching in Matthew 18. If someone has done you a wrong, then you are to go to him and seek to work things out. One of the first things I discovered in doing this was that frequently I was mistaken in my perception. What I thought was a wrong was not intended that way, or was not a wrong at all. Finding this out was a great relief both to the other person and to me. Yet if I had never gone to him, it might have become a major issue between us.

Another guiding statement in Scripture about our relations with others is in Matthew 5. Here our Savior says we should bless those who curse us and pray for those who despitefully use us. While this is contrary to our normal inclination, it can produce positive results.

Some time ago I received some letters from a man who thought I had wronged him. In these letters he questioned my motives and my integrity, and he did so in an abusive manner. I confess this irritated me. At first I answered the letters and tried to explain that what he alleged was not so. For my trouble I got back a point-by-point rejoinder that ended with even more criticism. I concluded that it would be fruitless to attempt to answer his accusations. When the next letter came, therefore, I sent it back with a note that I did not think he would want this kind of letter in our files. Unfortunately, he responded with a still more critical letter. He assured me that he wanted those letters in our files as a continuing indictment of me.

Some weeks later in my devotions, I read, "Pray for those who despitefully use you." The statement struck me with great force. I really did not want to pray for that man but I knew that this commandment was for me to obey. It seemed to stand out in bold letters in the text. While I had read the statement many times before, I knew that the Spirit of God on this

71

occasion was commending this message directly to me.

I have not seen the man from that day until now. I do not know whether there was any change in him. But I know what happened to me. As I began to pray for him, God healed my spirit. And today I do not have the anger toward that man that was building up within me. The sense of outrage and the desire to get even drained away as I began to practice what the Word of God taught me to do.

This reminds me of Ernest Gordon's book, *Through the Valley of the Kwai.* Gordon tells how an enlisted man asked him to read the Bible to him. This was after they both had been terribly mistreated by the Japanese. In fact I wept as I read about what happened when a shovel was missing. The Japanese officer asked who stole it, but no one responded. Then they were all threatened with severe punishment. At that, one man stepped forward and said that he would take the blame for the loss. Before them all, the Japanese officer beat him to death. Later, the shovel was found. The man really was innocent but because he believed the Bible taught that one should lay down his life for his friends, he took the penalty.

This was typical of the change that occurred as Gordon and the others sought to follow what Scripture taught. When a trainload of Japanese wounded came in to the station alongside their train, some British soldiers who had been so horribly mistreated by the enemy went over and ministered to the Japanese wounded, because they believed that this was what God wanted them to do. Gordon found that obedience to Scripture's commands can bring about a dramatic change in our attitudes and practices.

We need to remember also that we may sometimes be in too great a hurry to resolve a problem. Years ago I knew a young professor who developed an antipathy toward the administration of a college. A certain amount of this seems almost inevitable, but this man's feelings went much deeper. The situation had deteriorated to the point that other faculty and students were being affected. Obviously, something had to be done. Repeated conversations with the man produced no positive results. The only other alternative seemed to be to initiate action to discharge him.

At that point he submitted his resignation. Reportedly, he did this to force the issue, believing that the college administration could not afford to lose him. Not sharing this viewpoint, the administrative officers accepted his resignation. They did not have to discharge him. He did that himself.

Certainly there are occasions when a leader must act decisively. A crisis demands immediate action. But at other times it is appropriate to wait and let the Lord work the thing out, somewhat as Moses and the children of Israel did when they "stood still to see the salvation of the Lord."

This is what the manner of life of the Christian leader should be. It should manifest a conformity to the teachings of the Word of God. And it should reflect the indwelling presence and power of the Holy Spirit as he both discloses the will of God and enables the believer to do it.

CHAPTER SEVEN
LOVE AND PURITY
1 Corinthians 13

TWO OTHER ASPECTS of the profile of the believer—and thus of the Christian leader—are love and purity. To get an insight into the biblical concept of love, consider a statement by our Lord Jesus Christ in answer to a question posed to him by a lawyer. This is found in Matthew 22:35-40: "Then one of them, who was a lawyer, asked him a question, testing him, and saying, Master, which is the great commandment in the law? Jesus said unto him, Thou shalt love the Lord thy God with all thy heart, and with all thy soul, and with all thy mind. This is the first and great commandment. And the second is like unto it. Thou shalt love thy neighbor as thyself. On these two commandments hang all the law and the prophets."

Another definitive statement is in 1 John 4:7-11: "Beloved, let us love one another: for love is of God; and every one that loveth is born of God, and knoweth God. He that loveth not knoweth not God; for God is love. In this was manifested the love of God toward us, because that God sent his only begotten Son into the world, that we might live through him. Herein is love, not that we loved God, but that he loved us, and sent his Son to be the propitiation for our sins. Beloved, if God so loved us, we ought also to love one another."

It is not possible here to deal comprehensively with the

subject of love as recorded in the Bible. However, we should keep in mind the two major words that are translated "love" in the New Testament. These are probably best distinguished in the incident in John 21, where the Lord Jesus three times asked the Apostle Peter if he loved him. In the New International Version it is rendered this way: "Peter, do you truly love me?" "Yes, Lord, you know I love you." This translation has sought to distinguish between the two major words by rendering one "truly love" and the other "love."

The word we are considering is the one translated "truly love," which describes God's love. This word is in more than one hundred verses of the New Testament, and sometimes is used more than once in those verses. From these references we may gain an understanding of how the word is used in Scripture. It tells us something about the character of God. It also helps us to understand the meaning of the commandment to love God. If we are to be examples of the believers as far as love is concerned, this will be manifested as we love the Lord our God with all our heart and soul and mind and strength. In addition, we will gain insight as to how we are to express love to others, whether to the non-Christian or to the Christian.

Love is first and foremost a characteristic of God. When Scripture in Genesis 1:26 says, "Let us make man in our image," it suggests the Trinity, or *plurality in unity.* This doctrine sheds light on the expression "God is love." Since God existed before the universe came into being and before people were created, it follows that love was present in eternity past, even when nothing else was present.

If it is true that love requires an object—if it is to be truly love—what was there to be loved before the world existed? I believe the answer is that the members of the Trinity loved one another. Thus, in the very being of the Triune God are found the subjects and the objects of love, one loving the other. The Father loved the Son and the Holy Spirit. The Son loved the Father and the Holy Spirit. The Holy Spirit loved the Father and the Son. This interaction in the very being of God is simply stated: "God is love." This love did not have to wait until the creation of mankind to find its proper expression. It was and is inherent within the very nature and being of God himself.

Since the creation and the fall, God has wonderfully manifested his love toward us in redemption. Now it is our responsibility and privilege to love the Lord our God with all of our heart, soul, mind, and strength, as the first and great commandment specifies. The question is how we are to do this. Godly men and women have identified loving God as an act of worship, of spending time in his presence. While I do not discount this, I think Scripture suggests a far more specific way to indicate our love for God.

In John 14 we have a definitive statement about it. The Lord Jesus told his disciples (verses 15-18): "If ye love me, keep my commandments. And I will pray the Father, and he shall give you another Comforter, that he may abide with you for ever; Even the Spirit of truth; whom the world cannot receive, because it seeth him not, neither knoweth him: but ye know him; for he dwelleth with you, and shall be in you. I will not leave you comfortless: I will come to you." In verse 21 he continues: "He that hath my commandments, and keepeth them, he it is that loveth me: and he that loveth me shall be loved of my Father, and I will love him, and will manifest myself in him." Then in verse 23, in answer to Judas' question, Jesus said, "If a man love me, he will keep my words: and my Father will love him, and we will come unto him, and make our abode with him."

In these three references the Lord has emphasized the fact that love and obedience are inextricably intertwined. Thus, none of us can say we love the Lord and yet be disobedient to what he commands. If so, we really do not mean what we say. On the other hand, we express love to the Lord with all of our heart, soul, mind, and strength by keeping his commandments.

Love that is expressed in obedience to our Savior's

commands produces a remarkable result. We gain a depth and a comprehensiveness of understanding that we did not have before. The experience of happily married persons illustrates this. They fell in love, as the saying goes, and were married, but then as their love deepened, they found that there were wellsprings of understanding and insight in the other person that they had not seen at first.

This stands in contrast to an attraction that is purely external. A national news magazine described a well-known actress as a hollow woman with a beautiful shell. What a tragedy when there is only hollowness inside! But where there is love instead of the infatuation of the moment, there is a growing knowledge about the other individual. So it is in our love for the Lord that is expressed in obedience.

When our Savior said, "If you love me, keep my commandments," he immediately connected it with this statement: "And I will pray the Father and he will give you another Comforter, even the Spirit of Truth, that he may abide with you for ever." Thus our obedience to the Lord in keeping his commandments as an expression of our love for him is linked to the disclosure of truth through the ministry of the blessed Holy Spirit.

The same linkage between obedience and disclosure is in verse 21: "He that hath my commandments, and keepeth them, he it is that loveth me: and he that loveth me shall be loved of my Father, and I will love him, and will manifest myself to him." Here the Savior himself promises to manifest himself to those who in obedience express their love for him. As was true of Moses, we have validated our right to the Lord's special disclosure of himself that he graciously initiates toward those who obey him.

Again in verse 23 Jesus declared, "If a man love me, he will keep my words: and my Father will love him, and we will come unto him, and make our abode with him." One way to come to know others better is to live in their homes. Very quickly you will find out things about them you did not know before. People can wear a facade, but at home they show how they really are.

This passage also teaches that the disclosure involves each of the Persons in the Trinity. If someone loves the Lord and keeps his commandments, the Holy Spirit will minister as the Spirit of Truth, God the Son will manifest himself to the individual, and both the Son and the Father will come and take up their abode with him.

One of the marks of the believer, then, is an increasing awareness of the greatness and the glory of the Lord whom we serve. This in turn should deepen our love and make even more effective our obedience. This is as it should be. The absence of this awareness suggests a barrenness that is unnatural to vibrant Christian living.

In his reply to his questioner, the Lord continued by saying, "The second commandment is like unto it; ye shall love your neighbor as yourself." In Luke 10, the question was posed, "Who is my neighbor?" To answer that question, the Lord Jesus told the story of the Good Samaritan. This makes clear that our usual understanding of the term *neighbor* differs from that of our Savior's meaning of the word.

In the story of the Good Samaritan, the priest and the Levite looked at their fellow Jew in his need, and passed by on the other side. The Samaritan, on the other hand, ministered to him. So it is not national or geographical contiguity; it is not whether we live next door or in the same block. Our Savior's definition of neighbor is one whom we see to be in need. This transcends racial, cultural, and economic barriers; none of these is significant because the only criterion is need.

Often those who seek to apply the teaching of the parable of the Good Samaritan assume that the point is the meeting of physical need. Many earnest Christians believe we should be good neighbors by giving money or goods, or providing housing or job opportunities. So we should. But I believe that when our Savior gave this illustration of the man by the roadside who was terribly beaten and wounded, he did not intend that we should limit ourselves to the physical dimensions of human need. I am persuaded that our love for our neighbors is incomplete if we meet only their material and physical needs. To be sure, the meeting of such needs is an expression of love that often is necessary to manifest our concern. But if we stop at that point, our love for our neighbor is not comprehensive enough.

If we meet the temporal needs of men and do not meet their eternal needs, our action is akin to the individual who to keep warm chops up his furniture and burns it in the fireplace. He is warm for a time, but what does he do the next day? He has no furniture on which to sit or to place his food, and no more material to burn for warmth. Similarly, some have so concentrated on the tangible needs that they have not recognized the necessity of meeting both temporal and eternal needs. Furthermore, what is often overlooked is that the spiritual needs may be far more critical than the physical.

This reminds me of an experience I had in Jerusalem. After I checked into the hotel an Arab assisted me with my suitcases. Not knowing whether the service was added to the bill, or whether the man should be paid on the spot, I said, "I am very sorry. I have just arrived in the country and I do not have change to give you." The man looked at me with an expression I can still see and said, "Sir, I don't need money; I need hope."

This is the point. Many are wounded and bleeding inside. Too often we are like the priest and the Levite, passing by on the other side. We do not take the time required to deal with this kind of need. Instead, we find it easier to contribute money to meet material needs than to take the time to deal with the much more basic need of the individual.

I found this true during my active duty as a Navy officer. I had little difficulty insuring that the men of my division lived in clean quarters, had adequate food and clothing, and received the proper training. On the other hand, I found little opportunity to deal with their personal needs.

I well remember a young seaman. He couldn't have been more than seventeen. His buddies set out to introduce him to life. Every time they went ashore they endeavored to get him "fouled up" with alcohol and the wrong kind of women. Finally, one day one of the men remarked casually that they had at last succeeded in their plan and seemed pleased with their so-called accomplishment. I admit to becoming very angry and telling him exactly what I thought of what they had done. Yet no one else seemed to care. I attempted to do what I could, but I was limited by a lack of adequate opportunity to prevent what had happened. In retrospect, I wish I had taken the trouble to give him an alternative to the kinds of recreation and companions that were available. The best I could do afterward was to encourage a different way of life, realizing that I could not undo what had been done.

In Christian higher education I have had opportunity to meet some young people who had no shortage of money, experience, and opportunity; yet had terrible inner needs that were not being met. In virtually every case a major factor was a lack of parental love and discipline. For seemingly understandable reasons the parents provided lavishly for everything but what their child needed most. In this, their perception of need was defective and sometimes with tragic consequences.

So, who is your neighbor? He is the one in need. What is the need? It may be physical, but very often it is emotional and spiritual. It is the responsibility of the Christian leader to seek to meet that need.

To understand how to meet a need in love, we need a biblical pattern. We can find such a pattern in Hebrews 12, which says: "And ye have forgotten the exhortation which speaketh unto you as unto children, My son, despise not thou the chastening of the Lord, nor faint when thou art rebuked of him: For whom the Lord loveth he chasteneth, and scourgeth every son whom he receiveth. If ye endure chastening, God dealeth with you as with sons; for what son is he whom the father chasteneth not? But if ye be without chastisement, whereof all are partakers, then are ye illegitimate and not sons. Furthermore we have had fathers of our flesh which corrected us, and we gave them reverence; shall we not much rather be in subjection unto the Father of spirits, and live? For they verily for a few days chastened us after their own pleasure; but he for our profit, that we might be partakers of his holiness. Now no chastening for the present seemeth to be joyous, but grievous: nevertheless afterward it yieldeth the peaceable fruit of righteousness unto them which are exercised thereby."

This is a difficult passage for some to accept. How can the Lord love us if he chastens us? Scripture provides a sublime example of this in the action of the Heavenly Father toward his only begotten Son. There is no question but that the Father loved the Son. We know also from the prophecy of Isaiah, and from the New Testament, that the Lord has laid on him the iniquity of us all. Furthermore, in the garden our Savior prayed, "Oh, my Father, if it be possible, let this cup pass from me." Could such chastening be an evidence of the Father's love? It is. This becomes clear when we come to understand the purpose of it all.

This point comes out in Hebrews 5:8, which says: "Though he were a Son, yet learned he obedience by the things which he suffered; And being made complete, he became the author of salvation to as many as obey him." God the Father permitted his Son to have the experience of suffering in order that in some way which I do not comprehend, the Son might learn obedience by the things which he suffered, and, becoming complete, be the author of salvation to as many as obey him. I suggest that this is a principle that ought to be followed by the Christian who is an example of the believer in love as he deals with his fellow Christians.

Obviously this is in radical contrast to the popular concept of love. In fact, the word "love" has been so misused that it has virtually lost its meaning. Yet this need not be so in the Christian community. If we love one another, there may be occasions when loving action may hurt; but it will be for the good of the other person. As is true of God's loving chastening, it will enable the individual to be a partaker of his holiness, and to evidence the peaceable fruit of righteousness.

Despite the biblical encouragement to manifest this kind of love, we too often presume that it is more loving simply to pass by on the other side or to ignore what is going on. Our attitude seems to be, "That's his business. If he wants to do that, he should be allowed to do so." Occasionally I find that one of our fellowship is not living as he should. When I ask whether others knew about it, I find that they did. Then when I ask why no one went to the person in question to raise the issue, the reply I receive is, "Well, that was his business." That, I submit, is not Christian love, even though some might say that it was loving not to disturb or challenge another believer or to make him uncomfortable.

Scripture teaches the opposite. Consider this illustration in the second chapter of Galatians. In confronting his compromising brother in Christ, Paul "withstood him to his face, because he was to be blamed." This was an act of brotherly love on Paul's part—to save Peter from himself.

So if there are those under your direction who are doing things that are not right, it is not loving to condone their actions out of fear of being an intruder. Rather, "considering yourself, lest you also be tempted," go to the person in question and seek in humility to restore such a one.

I believe that this principle applies in the home as well as in the Christian community generally. The principle should relate both to husbands and wives and to parents and children. Admittedly, this is not as well accepted as it should be.

Years ago I visited a couple who were raising their children in accordance with the theories that were then current. They had accepted the notion that to correct a child would hurt his psyche. Avoiding correction, they set up a system of rewards as an incentive. For this they used a chart with gold stars. If the child ate his breakfast, he would get a star; if he brushed his teeth he would get another star.

82

On one occasion the mother shouted to the little boy as he rushed outside, "You're not going to get your gold star." In reply he called back, "I don't care about my gold star." That placed her in a dilemma, because she had no recourse but the gold star. Soon afterward, the other little boy came up behind me and hit me in the back as hard as he could. In what could be described as a conditioned reflex, I turned around, raised my hand, and struck him hard on what the doctors would call his *gluteus maximus.* He immediately retreated to a sanctuary under the bed and for quite a while refused to come out. But he never again hit me in the back.

I do not mean to suggest that I acted in love. My reaction was one of anger. Yet when correction is needed, it should be given promptly and firmly.

Once when I was in real difficulty and seemed unable to cope with my problem, some brothers in Christ visited me. They assured me that because they loved me, they thought it necessary to rebuke me. So they did. Ever since, I have been grateful to them, because only when they ministered to me in this way was I able to face the problem and deal with it. What really moved me was their attitude. Obviously, it was painful for them to do what they did. They showed real emotional stress. Yet in Christian love they refused to dismiss the matter as my personal business. Instead, they sought (in humility and with sensitivity, considering themselves lest they also be tempted) to be the spiritual ones who restored another in a spirit of meekness as an expression of their Christian love.

The ministry of example also includes purity. In Matthew 15 our Savior spoke directly to this matter: "And he called the multitude and said unto them, Hear, and understand: Not that which goeth into the mouth defileth a man: but that which cometh out of the mouth, this defileth a man. Then came his disciples, and said unto him, Knowest thou that the Pharisees were offended, after they heard this saying? But he answered and said, Every plant, which my heavenly Father hath not planted, shall be rooted up. Let them alone: they be blind leaders of the blind. And if the blind lead the blind, both shall fall into the ditch.

"Then answered Peter and said unto him, Explain unto us this parable. And Jesus said, Are ye also yet without understanding? Do not ye yet understand, that whatsoever entereth in at the mouth goeth into the stomach and is cast out into the draught? But those things which proceed out of the mouth come forth from the heart; and they defile the man. For out of the heart proceed evil thoughts, murders, adulteries, fornications, thefts, false witness, blasphemies: These are the things which defile a man: but to eat with unwashed hands defileth not a man" (Matthew 15:10-20).

Consider also our Lord's word in Matthew 6:24: "No man can serve two masters: for either he will hate the one and love the other; or else he will hold to the one and depise the other. Ye cannot serve God and mammon."

The word for purity is not used often in the New Testament. We find it only in 1 Timothy 4:12 and 5:2, where the reference is to treating the younger women as sisters, with all purity.

The basic meaning of the term "purity" is freedom from defilement. This can be understood in one of two ways. The first is freedom from uncleanness. This refers to the things mentioned by our Lord Jesus in Matthew 15—the evil thoughts which result in evil actions. The other use of the word conveys the thought of that which is unadulterated, as for example a singular loyalty that has no other commitment but one. Both of these meanings are pertinent to our being an example of the believers in purity, the purity of thought and the purity of commitment.

In the Sermon on the Mount the Lord Jesus spoke about purity of thought, saying: "Ye have heard that it was said by them of old time, Thou shalt not commit adultery; but I say unto you, That whosoever looketh on a woman to lust after her hath committed adultery with her already in his heart" (Matthew 5:27, 28). On the basis of this, I believe that in the Matthew 15 passage there should be a colon after "evil thoughts," because it is from evil thoughts that evil actions come, just as surely as night follows day.

Even within the Christian community, there is not a realistic understanding of this. For example, we heard recently of some Christians who went to Chicago to see an X-rated movie. They said they needed to be aware of what movies portrayed. Perhaps they returned unaffected by that experience, but I doubt it. Personally, I believe I should not see an X-rated movie or immerse my mind in scatological literature. I do not believe that such experiences are necessary in order to be well informed, particularly at the expense of a sullied mind.

In a conference of educators we were asked to read one of the books by Kurt Vonnegut, Jr., *Slaughterhouse Five.* Our discussion was led by a woman. When we were asked for our comments, I observed that while I was familiar with the language and the viewpoints portrayed, I questioned the choice of this kind of literature. I said I regretted that a woman would be asked to lead our discussion. In reply, she expressed her opinion that it is necessary to be aware of such things. My response was that I did not need to read *Slaughterhouse Five* to know that the people of the world are immoral and perverted in behavior, but I do need to guard my mind against mental impurity, in order to avoid impure acts.

At some points Scripture itself is more candid than some sensitive Christians would like. But Scripture is restrained in its descriptions and leaves no doubt about the wrongness of the action reported. I remember visiting an officer aboard another ship while I was overseas in World War Two. The first time I came to see him, he was expecting me. The next week I came back unexpectedly and found he had put back on the bulkheads the pictures he had taken down before my first visit. The pictures were calculated to incite lust. I could not help wondering what effect these pictures had upon him or upon those who came to his stateroom.

Sometimes such a practice is excused as mere mental daydreaming. But what about the current illegitimacy rate and the abortion rate? I believe these statistics suggest a correlation between unclean thinking and immoral action.

The Christian leader has a clear word from Scripture about mental purity: whatever things are true, honest, just, pure, lovely, and of good report—these are the things on which we should set our minds. Otherwise, we will not be an example of purity.

Consider also the purity expressed in singularity of commitment. One way to discover whether such commitment is present is to observe an individual between the time he resigns from an organization and the time he actually leaves it. Those with a purity of commitment will give full measure until the last day. The others will not. On this basis I have formulated references for those who later inquire about an individual who is no longer with us.

Let it not be said of us that the attraction of a new assignment causes us to do less than our very best in our present work. Rather, let us make sure that as examples of the believers in purity of commitment we shall do our job up to the moment of leaving.

This is to be expected because the singularity of our commitment is first of all to the Lord rather than to our career or to our own well-being. That being so, we have no option but to please him, for we are no longer our own. It is this kind of example of true discipleship that the Christian leader is expected to demonstrate.

CHAPTER EIGHT
FAITH
Hebrews 11:1-6; 8-19

BESIDES DEFINING WHAT A Christian leader should be, Scripture provides outstanding illustrations of the qualities that ought to characterize Christian leaders. One of these qualities is faith. The leader best known for this is Abraham.

Before considering Abraham, let us look at a definitive statement from Scripture on faith. Hebrews 11:1-6 in the New International Version says: "Now faith is being sure of what we hope for and certain of what we do not see. This is what the ancients were commended for. By faith we understand that the universe was formed at God's command, so that what is seen was not made out of what was visible. By faith Abel offered God a better sacrifice than Cain did. By faith he was commended as a righteous man, when God spoke well of his offerings. And by faith he still speaks, even though he is dead. By faith Enoch was taken from this life, so that he did not experience death; he could not be found, because God had taken him away. For before he was taken, he was commended as one who pleased God. And without faith it is impossible to please God, because anyone who comes to him must believe that he exists and that he rewards those who earnestly seek him."

This passage begins with a short definition of faith: "being sure of what we hope for and certain of what we do not see." Then it ends with a statement that suggests why faith is vital to our relationship with God: "And without faith it is impossible to please God, because anyone who comes to him must believe that he exists and that he rewards those who earnestly seek him."

The latter statement indicates that faith is incompatible with both atheism and deism. Those who come to God must believe that he exists. The verb is in the present tense. God is now a living reality rather than a historical curiosity. To have faith, one must hold this assumption or presupposition. This rules out atheism.

A number of prominent individuals in the Colonial and Revolutionary periods were deists. They believed in God but insisted that he was so distant from man that it was not possible for human beings to be in personal contact with him. They thought instead that whatever God wanted man to know could be seen in the natural creation and perceived by reason.

In more modern times, some theologians have spoken of God as being so wholly *other* that it is not possible to have any personal relationship with him. As a consequence, man is essentially left to himself.

In contrast to such notions, faith presumes that God exists today and is responsive to those who diligently seek him. Our Lord Jesus Christ affirmed this in the account recorded in Matthew 16. There, after Peter had made his great confession that Jesus was the Christ, the Son of the living God, Jesus said that flesh and blood had not revealed this to him but instead the Father in heaven had revealed it.

In other words, God the Father gave Peter the insight that the Man standing before him was Christ, the Son of the living God. This not only gives us a revelation about the person of Christ but also about the nature of God and of his communication with man. In fact, when our Savior said that flesh and blood did not reveal this to Peter, he meant that this knowledge came not by report nor observation nor by human speculation but by the revelation of God.

Faith then presumes that God communicates with man. It also presumes that God responds to faith. James Hudson Taylor is quoted as saying that it was not so much that we have faith, but that our faith is in a faithful God. Thus we believe in a God who is faithful and who is able to do "exceeding abundantly above all that we can ask or think." So while faith is important, it is important only because of the character of God.

In the passage we are considering there is also an indication of the comprehensiveness of faith. Referring to the past, Scripture says, "By faith we understand that the universe was formed at God's command, so that what is seen was not made out of what was visible" (Hebrews 11:3, NIV). By faith we know that creation, as theologians say, was made *ex nihilo,* brought out of nothing. God did not take existing material and form it into land and water. Matter is not eternal. Only God is eternal. He made the universe out of nothing. In fact, Scripture says, "He spoke and it was done." What a dramatic moment that must have been! Imagine God saying, "Be created," and the universe coming into being. That would have been something to see! But the writer of Hebrews says that the only way we know this happened is by faith. There is really no other satisfactory way of knowing how it all began. By faith we accept the fact that God spoke and it was done.

This passage also makes mention of man's present existence. The specific reference is to Abel, who was commended as a righteous man because he offered a better sacrifice. From this we may infer that faith is a working principle that can inform the life of the believing individual. Because Abel was sensitive to God, he made his offering by faith. In killing an animal from his flock he demonstrated his belief that the sacrifice would be significant in God's sight. Thus Abel lived by faith.

Finally, this Scripture uses an illustration of how faith relates to the future. "By faith Enoch was taken from this life, so that he did not experience death." Hence, faith in Christ and eternal life are inextricably linked together. With the poet the Christian can say: "Life is real, Life is earnest. And the grave is not its goal. 'Dust thou art, to dust returnest' was not spoken of the soul."

Thus by the Holy Spirit the writer of Hebrews gives us an insight into what faith is. By definition, faith is being sure of what we hope for and certain of what we do not see. It is rooted in the character of a self-existent and self-revealing God. It is pertinent to understanding the past, living responsibly in the present, and possessing hope for the future. Therefore, faith comprehensively relates to the whole of life and has as its object a faithful God.

With that in mind, let us consider Abraham as a man of faith. Scripture describes him this way: "By faith Abraham, when called to go to a place he would later receive as his possession, obeyed and went, even though he did not know where he was going. By faith he made his home in the promised land like a stranger in a foreign country; he lived in tents, as did Isaac and Jacob, who were heirs with him of the same promise. For he was looking forward to the city with foundations, whose architect and builder is God. By faith Abraham, even though he was past age—and Sarah herself was barren—was enabled to become a father because he considered him faithful who had made the promise. And so from this one man, and he as good as dead, came descendants as numerous as the stars in the sky and as countless as the sand of the seashore" (Hebrews 11:8-12, NIV).

Another part of the same chapter says, "By faith Abraham, when God tested him, offered Isaac as a sacrifice. He who had received the promises was about to sacrifice his one and only son, even though God had said to him, 'Through Isaac shall your promised offspring come.' Abraham reasoned that God could raise the dead. Figuratively speaking, he did receive Isaac back from death" (Hebrews 11:17-19, NIV).

In making a case study of Abraham as an illustration of the man of faith, we should note two major emphases: Abraham's exercise of faith in dealing with material things, and his exercise of faith in dealing with other persons. In both instances he acted in accordance with God's promises to him.

In Genesis 12 we read that the Lord told Abraham: "Get thee out of thy country, and from thy kindred, and from thy father's house, unto a land that I will shew thee: And I will make of thee a great nation, and I will bless thee, and make thy name great; and thou shalt be a blessing: and in thee shall all families of the earth be blessed."

Abraham obeyed this command and went out, "not knowing where he went." When he came into the land, there the Lord added to what he had originally said to Abraham: "Unto thy seed will I give *this* land."

At this point Abraham was put to the test. That is generally what happens in the walk of faith. A commandment is obeyed by faith. As a result, God gives more light. Then faith is tested.

In the case of Abraham this came when a disagreement developed between Lot's herdsmen and his. Then Abraham was faced with a dilemma. While God had promised him this land, his herdsmen and those of his nephew could not get along. So he had two alternatives: to tell Lot to get out or to let Lot choose what he wanted.

As a man of faith, Abraham was willing to allow Lot to choose because he believed that God was going to honor his promise to give him the land. In the meantime, whether Lot chose the land was not of major consequence. The promise was still there. When Abraham had passed the test of faith, then the Lord gave him this reassurance: "Lift up now thine eyes, and look from the place where thou art northward, and southward, eastward, and westward: all the land which thou seest, to thee will I give it, and to thy seed for ever" (Genesis 13:14, 15).

The Lord had tested Abraham by asking, in effect, "Do you really believe my promise?" When Abraham showed that he trusted in God's sovereign power by letting Lot choose, then the Lord commended Abraham and promised to give him all that he could see. This suggests that to have faith one must believe in the promise of God to such a degree that the intermediate maneuverings and changes will make no difference in his confidence about the ultimate purposes of God. This is what the writer of Hebrews had in mind when he said, "These all died in faith, not having received the promises but having seen them afar off and were persuaded of them and embraced them and confessed that they were strangers and pilgrims in the earth. For they that say such things declare plainly that they seek a country."

Some years ago we were ministering at a weekend retreat. Toward the end of our time together one of the group asked if he could talk privately with me. Then he explained his problem. He was heavily in debt and had been manipulating his accounts so that his creditors and the bank would not know of his desperate financial condition. For a time this seemed to work, but finally his obligations became too heavy. He said he was afraid to go to the bank because he was sure that if he told them the truth they would call in his notes and he would be bankrupt and disgraced. Then he asked, "What shall I do? How can I take care of my wife and children?"

After discussing this for a while I told him that even though it might seem difficult, he should do the right thing and trust God to take care of him afterward. By acting honestly, he would honor God, and God would not be unmindful of his obedience and trust.

He thanked me for my counsel, but he was still a miserable man. Although he had not been living by faith, but by his own clever devices, he was painfully aware of the fact that his affairs were a mess. I promised to pray for him. Soon the conference was over. A few weeks later his wife wrote to tell me what happened. One evening the whole family got on their knees in the living room and prayed that the Lord would give the husband and father the strength and the courage to do what he knew was right. Then he went to the bank and asked for an appointment with the president. He confessed that he had been deceiving him for many months and that he was now in a financial crisis. Then he outlined his problem.

After he had finished talking, the president of the bank told him he was willing to give him a chance because he believed that my friend would not have come to him if he did not have something in his character that was worthy of confidence. Then he worked out a line of credit for him and a system whereby he could pay his debts.

The following spring when I saw him again, he was a changed man. No longer did he have to manipulate his accounts or worry whether he would be found out. Instead, he believed that when he obeyed God by being honest and forthright in his financial dealings, he could count on the providence of God.

We should be careful to note that obeying God does not always result in material benefits. Jim Vaus, the gambler who came to know the Lord, determined to pay those to whom he felt obligated. When he drove his Cadillac downtown to deliver it to the new owner, he did not know whether he had enough gasoline to get to his destination—and had no money to buy more. But having become a Christian, he believed that God wanted him to pay his bills, and as far as possible to right the wrongs that he had done. When he went back to his house that had been sold, with all the furniture gone and no rugs on the floor, he experienced peace even though he was penniless. His was a practical trust in God, even though he would no longer have his Cadillac or his beautiful home.

On the other hand, what we do in faith by obeying the Lord may sometimes produce surprising consequences. Recently I heard of a man who had been bribing a contractor because he understood this was the only way to get business for his firm. Even though he was a Christian he paid the bribes over a period of three years. Finally, his conscience convicted him so about this dishonest practice that he decided he would do it no more, contracts or no contracts. He went to the contractor's office and said, "I have a confession to make. Even though I haven't acted like one, I am a Christian. I know it is wrong for me to pay you these bribes for my contracts. So, I am not going to do it anymore, even if I lose all of your business."

To his surprise, the contractor burst into tears and told him he had been using the money from the bribes to finance a double life. "I have been hoping that somehow I could stop," he said. "I thank God that I won't be getting any more bribes. This will help me change my behavior."

Can you imagine what it did to the businessman to realize that in the midst of a system characterized by bribes and under-the-counter dealings, he could glorify God by resolving to believe and trust him?

Living by faith can be characteristic of institutions as well as individuals. At Wheaton we determined not to take available aid from the national or state governments for operational expenses. Only a few colleges in Illinois hold this conviction. A number of Christian colleges take such aid. While we recognize this is a matter for each college to decide, the reason we do not take government grants to pay for operational expenses is our conviction that this keeps us free to be pervasively Christian in our programs and practices.

In a recent Supreme Court ruling, decided by a 5 to 4 vote, one of the major points is that a school can divide its program into "sacred" and "secular" elements. For those that are secular it is legitimate to receive national and state aid. We at Wheaton, on the other hand, believe that the life of the *entire* campus should be under the lordship of Christ and the authority of Holy Scripture, including our business affairs, our advertising, our athletics, and the integration of faith and learning in our classrooms.

This means that we forego hundreds of thousands of dollars that we might obtain from the national or state government for new construction or for operational grants-in-aid. Yet in extraordinary ways the college has experienced the validity of

J. Hudson Taylor's statement: "God's work, done in God's way, will never lack God's supply." I believe the college is solvent today because we have sought to trust in God for the supply of our needs. And as we make honest effort to integrate faith and learning in all aspects of campus life, we are confident we will endure as long as God wants us to be in existence. We will continue to function even though we do not take grants from the national or state governments.

Abraham is an illustration to us of how to have confidence in God so that even when times of testing come, we may trust in him and then see him act. The tests of our faith may take a number of forms. Consider these in the life of Abraham. When Lot chose the best land, Abraham might well have felt that their relationship had come to an end. But he did not. And when five kings overran Sodom and carried Lot away, Abraham defeated them to rescue Lot. Then when the heavenly visitors told Abraham they were going to destroy Sodom, he interceded for his nephew and may very well have been instrumental in his being spared.

All this was because Abraham, as a man of faith, trusted in God and was therefore at liberty to help his nephew, even though Lot was greedy for immediate gain. As a man of faith, Abraham could still show love toward his nephew because he had no need to be concerned about what he was going to gain or lose in this situation.

We should remember, however, that in Egypt and at Gerar, this giant of the faith showed that he did not always live consistently. Abraham's problem lay in Sarah's beauty. In these incidents we have an example of failure to apply the principle of faith consistently. Although God had met Abraham's needs for land and possessions, the patriarch still became fearful and unbelieving when personal relationships were involved. So he resorted to a contrivance. He called his wife his sister.

These experiences suggest an important truth to us. The exercise of faith is not like a diamond that keeps its quality forever. It is perishable. Unless our faith is constantly renewed, we too may go down to Egypt and to Gerar and find out how little faith we really have. I believe that God in sovereign providence allowed this to happen to Abraham so that he might recognize his need of complete dependence on God, rather than upon his faith. His faith and ours must be in God, not in our faith as such.

Another major test of Abraham's faith came in connection with the birth of Isaac. In considering this, we need to recognize that we are also confronting the issue of miracles. Even in the evangelical world, some who accept segments of Scripture that have to do with our salvation and our eternal destiny think that in matters of history, science, or chronology the Bible contains mistakes. Naturally, that creates a problem with miracles.

I do not subscribe to that point of view. I believe that one must accept all of Scripture, including its accounts of miracles. I believe what the Bible says—that Sarah was barren and that Abraham because of his age probably no longer could father a child. It was therefore the more incredible for God to promise Abraham and Sarah a son when they both knew very well that this was impossible. In fact, they found this so amusing that they laughed. Despite Sarah's subsequent denial, she thought it ridiculous that the strangers who made the announcement to her and Abraham apparently did not know that after a certain age women could not bear children.

In confronting this test of faith as to whether God could act in this way, Abraham and Sarah attempted to help God out. In effect they assumed that God needed some more natural or normal way to fulfill his covenant promise. So they sought to take care of the matter by having Hagar become Abraham's second wife. Out of that relationship was born Ishmael, the apparent solution to what seemed an impossible situation.

This happening dramatically illustrates that when we move from faith to presumption, the results are tragic. We need only look at the Middle East today to see the consequences existing over the centuries and persisting now in the conflict between Jew and Arab. The lesson is clear. If God has made a promise we think is impossible, our part is to place our faith in God, and not try to figure out ways in which we may help him out of his supposed dilemma.

At Drew University some years ago, I reviewed a program on the United Nations that Drew was offering. One of their staff came to me and said he understood I was from Wheaton. Then he said he was involved in an evangelistic campaign allegedly conducted by one of our graduates some years before. He said that when it came time for the invitation, the evangelist wanted to make sure that people would come forward, so he hired a number of college students who, as soon as the invitation was given, were to get up out of their seats and walk down to the front. In this way they would "prime the pump," and then others would come. As he told me this, I was reluctant to believe it, but he insisted that it was true.

Perhaps it was, in light of a report one of our sons gave about the way in which an evangelistic group handled a meeting he attended. The leader asked everyone to bow in prayer and then invited those present to receive Christ. Then he said, "Thank you, I see your hand, I see your hand." Out of curiosity our son had not shut his eyes. He saw no hands raised at that time. Yet the evangelist kept saying, "I see your hand," and eventually a few hands went up.

What could be the possible rationalization for such a procedure? In effect any person who thus manipulates others is saying that the Spirit of God cannot move people without contrivance. That seemed to be Abraham's and Sarah's point of view.

After Isaac's birth, Abraham faced another test of faith with which every father can identify. I have thought about this and imagined taking our son, Taylor, by the hand and saying, "Taylor, we are going for a walk up the mountain." He would say, "You have a knife and some wood and matches. Why are we taking these up the mountain?" "Son, we are going to offer a sacrifice." "But, Daddy, we have the wood and the matches, and the knife, but we don't have any lamb for the sacrifice."

At that point I suspect I would get so choked up that I could say no more. That is why I admire Abraham's being able to say, "My son, God will provide himself a lamb." To me, this is an amazing illustration of faith. Abraham obeyed without question when he got the perplexing command from God to take his only son, the one who was to be the fulfillment of God's promises, and offer him on the mountain.

Why was Abraham able to have such confidence? I think he reasoned that a God who could take the bodies of Sarah and himself and make them productive again was capable of performing another miracle in the body of Isaac. So he was willing to obey God.

Furthermore, Abraham really did not have an option in Ishmael. The New International Version renders Hebrews 11:17 this way: "He who had received the promises was about to sacrifice his one and only son." In this situation Ishmael did not count. Isaac was the only one, Abraham's only option.

We should thank God that the faith of Abraham, as Romans 4 tells us, can be our faith as well. Both in Romans 4 and in Galatians 3, statements about Abraham make the point that the kind of faith that Abraham exercised is the kind by which you and I pass from spiritual death to spiritual life. And then, when by faith we become children of Abraham, we should manifest the same quality of faith that he had in trusting God for Isaac's restoration to life. Even as a spiritually dead person can be made spiritually alive, so a spiritually vital person can live in obedience, trusting completely in a faithful God.

The Christian leader, in particular, must recognize that even if his professional future is at stake, or his relationships with other people are an issue, he must first of all be obedient to the commandments and the purposes of God. He must trust the sovereign Lord to work out all things after the counsel of his own will.

The evangelical world needs to see this kind of faith manifested today because even among Christians there is the temptation to manipulate others, ostensibly to strengthen their faith, by other than legitimate means.

Some years ago I was in a meeting of a group of Christians who had been involved in calling a new leader for their organization. Their chairman came into the meeting with an airmail special delivery letter. Before opening the letter, he asked the group to pray that they might accept whatever was in it. So everyone prayed. Then he dramatically opened the letter, read it, and said, "Praise God, he is coming." We all rejoiced. God had answered our prayers. It was an inspiring moment.

Months later I asked the man who had been chosen about his letter of acceptance. Quite casually he remarked that earlier in the day on which the letter was received, he had called that chairman and told him he was coming. I was disillusioned. The incident had been manufactured, with the supposed justification that we needed to have our faith buttressed by a device.

In all our relationships with others, we should be known as people who trust God and obey his Word. Any losses or setbacks we may experience are, in my judgment, more than compensated for by being right with God. As you maintain your integrity, he will work out his purpose for his glory and for your benefit.

CHAPTER NINE
SHAPING A LEADER
Acts 7:20-36
Hebrews 11:23-29

MOSES WAS ONE OF THE GREAT LEADERS in biblical history. Two sections of God's Word provide excellent summaries of his life. The first of these is in Acts 7, where Moses is mentioned in part of Stephen's sermon. The second is in Hebrews 11, where Moses is included in the list of the heroes of faith.

The statement in Acts is as follows: "Moses was born, and was exceeding fair [another translation puts it "a beautiful child"], and nourished up in his father's house three months: And when he was cast out, Pharoah's daughter took him up, and nourished him as her own son. And Moses was learned in all the wisdom of the Egyptians, and was mighty in words and in deeds. And when he was forty years old, it came into his heart to visit his brethren the children of Israel. And seeing one of them suffer wrong, he defended him, and avenged him that was oppressed, and smote the Egyptian: for he supposed his brethren would have understood how that God by his hand would deliver them: but they understood not. And the next day he shewed himself unto them as they strove, and would have set them at one again, saying, Sirs, ye are brethren; why do ye wrong one to another? But he that did his neighbor wrong thrust him away, saying, Who made thee a ruler and a judge over us? Wilt thou kill me, as thou didst the Egyptian yesterday? Then fled Moses at this saying, and was a stranger in the land of Midian, where he begat two sons. And when forty years were expired, there appeared to him in the wilderness of Mount Sinai an angel of the Lord in a flame of fire in a bush.''

In Hebrews 11 we read: "By faith Moses, when he was born, was hid three months by his parents, because they saw he was a beautiful child; and they were not afraid of the king's commandment. By faith Moses, when he was come to years, refused to be called the son of Pharaoh's daughter; choosing rather to suffer affliction with the people of God, than to enjoy the pleasures of sin for a season; esteeming the reproach of Christ greater riches than the treasures in Egypt; for he had respect unto the recompence of the reward. By faith he forsook Egypt, not fearing the wrath of the king: for he endured, as seeing him who is invisible. Through faith he kept the passover, and the sprinkling of blood, lest he that destroyed the firstborn should touch them. By faith they passed through the Red Sea as by dry land, which the Egyptians attempting to do were drowned.''

We shall consider these aspects of the life of Moses: his preparation in natural gifts, in spiritual enduement, and in experience. Then we shall also consider his actions in administration, in response to rejection and to sin, and his accountability.

A leader is one who has natural endowments. Scripture says that when Moses was born he was a beautiful child who was specially favored in the sight of the Lord. God endowed him with qualities requisite to leadership. One of these qualities was a higher than average intellect. Scripture says that he was skilled in all the wisdom of the Egyptians. His superior intellect could grasp Egypt's very considerable knowledge.

Another of Moses' endowments was a feeling of concern. Still another was a decisiveness in action. When he saw one of the Israelites being beaten, his emotions were aroused. This showed that he was able to be moved by injustice, a reaction requisite to true leadership. Furthermore, he had a sense of the dynamic of the moment that made him a true leader. As a result, he acted decisively. Perhaps there might have been a better way, but Moses decided the only way to defend his countryman was to attack the Egyptian and kill him.

To be sure, decisiveness may be carried too far. The late John Foster Dulles traveled so extensively around the world that someone suggested the President should have told him, "Don't just do something; stand there!" Yet the usual problem is that we are immobilized by indecision; we don't know what to do or how to do it. I prefer someone who acts even if on occasion he makes mistakes. I believe that if he is 51 percent right in his actions he is performing more satisfactorily than if he does nothing.

Moses also possessed spiritual capabilities. Scripture says that when he was come to years he chose rather to suffer affliction with the people of God, than to enjoy the pleasures of sin for a season. It says also that he esteemed the reproach of Christ greater riches than the treasures in Egypt.

The Christian leader must determine that he will go God's way and not make his decisions on the basis of such considerations as his relationship with the hierarchy, or his financial reward, or his status. Furthermore, he must be spiritually discerning in his willingness to identify himself with the people of God.

An admiral who was a Christian once suggested that in going to a new assignment, the first thing to do is to run up your flag, to indicate your identity with Jesus Christ. In this crisis of allegiance, Moses ran up his flag. He chose to reject the option of going with the prevailing culture. He spurned the current climate of opinion. Instead he identified himself with the despised minority. Scripture says he did this because he endured as seeing him who is invisible, and because he considered the reward that was in the future for him. In other words, he had a spiritual perspective—a clear-eyed vision of the One whom he served and of the eternal recompense that only he could give.

At this point in his experience, because of the killing of the Egyptian, Moses had to leave Egypt and spend forty years in the back side of the desert. This experience of Moses' suggests a generalization which may have exceptions but which has significant scriptural support. I believe that in choosing people for leadership God waits until the person in question is ready. In Moses' case, God waited forty years until the pride and desire for status and all the other things characteristic of Egypt were put in their proper place. During that time Moses learned patience and humility and the ability to step aside and have no status whatsoever. I do not believe that Moses expected ever again to return to the status he previously had.

It is one thing to become successful. It is quite another to go down after having been up. This is one of the qualities God seeks in the life of the leader. Is he capable on the basis of principle to go into isolation and obscurity for the cause for which he has given himself? Can he endure God's test to determine the quality of his dedication?

Remember that even our Lord Jesus Christ was about thirty years of age when he began his public ministry. We might explain this by saying that if he had started any sooner, he would not have been accepted in that culture. Perhaps this is so. Yet I believe that in some mysterious way, even our Savior in his humanity had to wait thirty years, after humbling himself to become a man, before he was ready to begin his public ministry.

So the first generalization is that God will select us for a task only when we are ready and prepared for the position he has for us.

The second generalization may be more difficult to accept. As I read Scripture, it seems to me that it is God who summons the leader to the position rather than the leader who seeks the opportunity.

Moses was not looking for a place of leadership. In fact, he needed considerable persuading to go back to Egypt. He went only because God opened the way and promised to be with him. The Lord knew that the circumstances were just right and that he could use Moses for his glory.

The experience of Joseph provides another illustration of this idea. After the dreams that predicted a leadership role, he faced one setback after another. If anything, the circumstances seemed to contradict his dreams. Yet at just the right time in history God opened the way for Joseph to assume the promised leadership role. Clearly, only the Lord could have ordered circumstances in such a way.

In my own career, the striking thing has been that I have yet to seek a position. When I left the Navy to go to graduate school to prepare for the mission field, I was offered a part-time teaching position at Wheaton, which I accepted. Later I was approached to go to Gordon College. While there I received an invitation to minister in a church in New Hampshire.

The New Hampshire invitation came about in an interesting way. I had gone to the campus to pick up my mail when the librarian just "happened," as we would say, to step out into the hall and see me. He said that his cousin had just called from Manchester, New Hampshire, to say that their pastor had suffered a heart attack. Then he asked if I would be willing to minister there for three or four Sundays. I agreed. Each Lord's Day the family and I drove to Manchester. After four weeks we said good-bye to the people there, as the pastor seemed sufficiently recovered to resume his duties. But within a month they called us again, told us that the pastor had suffered a second heart attack, and asked if we would come back. We did. In early May the pastor died.

We were scheduled to sail for China that summer, but had no housing until the time we were to leave. So we moved into the parsonage. When conditions in China prevented our sailing, the church asked us to remain even while we commuted from Manchester to Harvard to study Chinese.

When our mission asked us to resign because their missionaries were being withdrawn from China, the president of Gordon College offered me another position on the faculty. We moved to Brockton, Massachusetts, and began attending Trinity Baptist Church there. In the spring of 1951, the pastor told me he had resigned and asked if I would preach for a few Sundays until the church could call another minister. I told him I would be glad to fill in. So I preached for four months while the church contacted several ministers, all of whom turned them down. Finally in September they asked whether I would continue if they hired a full-time assistant. I agreed and continued for three and a half years, preaching in the church on Sundays and working at the College on weekdays. Despite the stress of those years, I learned many valuable lessons.

During that time Gordon's president asked me to serve as acting dean of the college for three months. I agreed to try. In May he requested that I continue as dean, which I did for ten years.

Then when he died and a new president was appointed, we were visited by Dr. Edman from Wheaton College. Just as he was leaving campus I happened to remark that I thought the Lord was "lifting the cloud" at Gordon, although I did not know where we were going. He responded by asking me to come to Wheaton and teach. After much prayer I accepted. When I had taught at Wheaton for a year and a half, Dr. Edman asked me to become his administrative assistant in academics, and less than two years later I was advised that the board of trustees were considering me for the presidency of Wheaton, an office I assumed in 1965.

I have had similar experiences with the presidency of the National Association of Evangelicals and of the World Evangelical Fellowship. I mention these things simply to say that in our experience God graciously has provided opportunities which we did not seek, but which he made available to us. We can always trust the providence of God for assignments that are right for us.

Consider now the third generalization: when God called Moses in the back side of the desert, he was dramatically different from the person he had been in Egypt. One version of Scripture describes him as having been mighty in words and in deeds when he was in Egypt. But when the Lord called him forty years later, Moses pointed out that he was slow of speech and of tongue. This might be explained as the result of not having talked much for forty years, and of not having shouldered any demanding leadership responsibilities during those decades. For whatever reason, he needed special enablement for the work God was calling him to do.

To accommodate Moses' fears, the Lord designated Aaron to be his mouthpiece. Early in the Exodus account it speaks of "Aaron and Moses," but soon it changes to "Moses and Aaron." This was because Moses increasingly did the speaking. And he acquired not simply an ability to be articulate but the capacity to utter an authoritative word of leadership. When God calls an individual and gives him a job to do, he will supernaturally provide the capabilities needed for that specific job.

In summary, then, a leader has both natural and supernatural gifts. He is prepared by God for just the right moment to assume his leadership role. When that time comes, God will open the door of opportunity. God will also provide whatever special enduements are necessary to that calling. The leader's responsibility is to be available, teachable, and responsible in fulfilling the assignment God gives.

In Moses' experience we also see an example of the way in which a leader should be able to delegate responsibility and not try to do too many things himself. Exodus 18 provides a case study in management technique. Jethro's visit to Moses suggests an important factor in administrative work, that is, the value of a management consultant. Admittedly, some consultants are much better than others; but much of the value springs from the detached perspective. That is what happened here. Jethro immediately saw the problem of people standing in line all day to present their controversies to Moses for an answer from him. By the end of the day Moses no doubt showed weariness because he had been so much in demand.

One of the perils in administrative leadership is the tendency to become caught up in the minutia of the job, and then to be unable to view things in perspective so as to deal with the major concerns of the enterprise. This is why Jethro urged Moses to appoint qualified men to be his subordinates.

Exodus 18:21 furnishes the basic qualifications for appointment. Moses was to employ associates who (1) feared God; (2) were men of truth; (3) hated covetousness. These are excellent criteria by which to select qualified subordinates today too. Those who must employ non-Christians may object that such individuals do not fear God. Yet even among non-Christians there are those who have high moral and ethical standards. There may at least be a respect for God or a willingness to acknowledge his sovereignty.

It is an obvious advantage to have associates who will speak and live the truth. It is an administrative blight to be told what others think you want to hear, rather than what really is. Men of truth not only speak the truth in dealing with an issue, but speak the truth to their superiors. Yet to speak the truth there must be a criterion of truth to which to relate the specific issues.

The theologian Dooyeweerd of the Netherlands is reported to have recommended that Christians read the Scriptures so regularly and with such understanding as to soak themselves in Scripture. When any particular issue confronts a Scripture-soaked individual he will be able immediately to think biblically and to apply pertinent Scriptural principles to the specific problem.

The third criterion is hating covetousness. This is a comprehensive matter. We usually think of covetousness as a problem generated by a love of money. But it includes more. Some leaders have had subordinates who so coveted their position that they were prepared to discredit their superior just as Absalom did David. I distinguish this from a natural ambition to better one's self and to be prepared for the next higher position. Rather, covetousness in this context is an inordinate ambition that constantly depreciates the leader so that the subordinate can appear more and more as *the* man for the situation. An identifying phrase often is: *if only.* "If only I were president; if only I were the pastor; if only I were the manager—I would take care of things as they should be treated." As in the case of Absalom, such covetousness results in an endeavor to steal away the hearts of the people. The leader therefore should choose subordinates who will not be covetous in this way but will serve effectively in their particular echelon.

Qualified subordinates are essential for the success of any enterprise. Fortunate indeed is the leader whose colleagues love truth and hate covetousness.

Notice that when he appointed subordinates this did not invalidate Moses' responsibility for basic policy. Verse 20 specifies: "Thou shalt teach them ordinances and laws, and shalt shew them the way wherein they must walk, and the work that they must do." This is done in two ways. The leader is responsible to enunciate general policy and also to provide management training.

For years I was content to set basic policy, assuming that the management knew their jobs. Then when I took some management training myself I came to realize the necessity of having the administrative group know procedures as well as policies. On this basis they could establish their priorities and achieve the general objectives.

I have found this procedure helpful. Each year I construct a series of goals for myself. At the end of the year I share with my key subordinates my appraisal of my own performance and ask for their perspective on this performance. Then I give them what I perceive to be appropriate goals for the coming year and ask them in turn to share these with their subordinates; in this way, the goals I eventually set will be the collective responsibility of the management team, not just of the president. Thus when I work on my goals I have the support of the vice presidents and of their subordinates working together as a team.

That is what I think Moses did. He established the objectives and the goals for the group, shared them with his associates, and instructed them so that they would know how to carry out the general policies he had established. Keep in mind that this does not relieve the leader of ultimate accountability. It simply means that by delegation he can do his work better.

This also makes more time available. Yet the saved time must be guarded or it can easily be dissipated. I have adopted this procedure. I do not take any phone calls from 8:00 to 9:00 in the morning. I reserve that time to plan the day and to think about the best way to use the rest of my time and energies. It is helpful daily to ask yourself what are the matters that only you can handle? If there is anything that anyone else can do, don't do it yourself. Give others freedom to do those things even if in some cases you could do them better yourself. I have had to tell myself that I am not going to be in my job indefinitely, and that others should learn to take responsibility. They should learn even about the functions that are mine alone, so that in an emergency they can handle them effectively.

In addition, subordinates should be told that they will be supported in the event that they make a mistake, as long as they understand that continuing to make the same mistakes will not be tolerated. Instead, they should learn from their mistakes and then make whatever corrections are necessary to keep from repeating the same mistake.

I have defended my subordinates even in costly mistakes because I had delegated the responsibility to them. Delegation carries with it both authority and accountability. Thus it is not right to be looking over a subordinate's shoulder or to take over for him when he falters. I am sure that when Moses delegated to others while keeping the major things for himself, if one of the subordinates made a decision with which Moses might not have agreed, he still permitted it to stand unless it was so contrary to basic policy that it had to be overruled. Certainly Moses would not have tolerated any indulgence of idolatry, for instance; but quite probably he permitted discretion in matters over which there could be an honest difference of opinion.

What is important in the matter of delegation is a periodic review. Even the best of us need this. A friend of mine says that most people do not do what they are *ex*-pected to do; they do what they are *in*-spected to do. Like any generalization, this one has its notable exceptions; but it is interesting how easily most of us slacken off when nobody is noticing, and how quickly we recover when we know someone is going to review our work. Certain exceptional people work well independently without being reviewed, but many people will make an extra effort when they know somebody is coming by to see them.

Both my military and my educational experience confirm this. I find that preparation for board meetings, when my performance is reviewed, is good for me. At such times some things that might have been overlooked get appropriate consideration. Thus, a periodic audit is good for all of us.

Moses also showed outstanding leadership qualities in the way in which he responded to Israel's sinful behavior and their rejection of him. Exodus 32 gives us the description of a series of circumstances that disclose the depth and scope of his devotion not only to the Lord but also to the children of Israel. To be sure, the circumstances are not unique. They have occurred in the lives of others who have been called to Christian leadership. But Moses' example here is an inspiring one for us all.

While he was still on the mountain with the Lord, Moses learned what was going on in the camp, so he was not surprised when he returned. He knew very well that the people were disobedient. They had rejected both him and the things for which he stood. More significantly, he knew Israel was acting contrary to the law that God had just given to him.

The remarkable thing to me is that before Moses left the mountain and after he had been made aware of the fact that the people had rejected him, God put him to the test. Verses 9 and 10 describe this test. Note especially the last phrase in verse 10: "Now therefore let me alone, that my wrath may burn against them, and that I may consume them; and I will make of thee a great nation."

Notice the temptation here. Moses had just been told that the people he had been leading in the wilderness had repudiated the things for which he stood and had become disobedient. Then God offered to make of him a great nation. In response Moses manifested one of his great capabilities, that of utilizing spiritual perspective. He was able to see things in proportion. His outlook was not so provincial or circumscribed that he saw everything in the light of his own interest. If anything foreshortens perspective and limits vision, it is personal ambition. So many considerations become blurred when everything else is set aside in favor of a preoccupation with personal ambition.

I once knew a man who had an illicit passion. It was astonishing the chances he took and the things he did. He seemed to have lost his judgment because of his inordinate desire for self-gratification. In Moses' case the temptation was in a more legitimate area, but was still a test to determine whether his personal ambition would distort his perspective.

We can rejoice in how gloriously Moses passed the test. Here is how Scripture describes it: "For Moses besought the Lord his God, and said, Lord, why doth thy wrath burn against thy people, whom thou hast brought forth out of the land of Egypt with great power, and with a mighty hand? Wherefore should the Egyptians speak, and say, For mischief did he bring them out, to slay them on the mountains, and to consume them from the face of the earth? Turn from thy fierce wrath, and repent of this evil against thy people. Remember Abraham, Isaac, and Israel, thy servants, to whom thou didst swear by thine own self, and said unto them, I will multiply your seed as the stars of heaven, and all this land that I have spoken of will I give to your seed, and they shall inherit it for ever."

Notice how completely detached from personal ambition Moses was. Even when he was offered a most remarkable possibility, he viewed it in light of the Lord's great covenant promises to his people, and of their reputation. Thus he in effect said to God, "Thank you very much, but I would plead with you not to do what you have suggested." That is the mark of a spiritually minded leader whose own ambition does not distort his perception of God's purposes for the enterprise in which he is involved.

To understand Moses' behavior when he came down from the mountain, we need to keep in mind the real meaning of the description in Numbers 12:3: "Now the man Moses was very meek." This meekness stands in contrast to the popular conception of meekness. When I was a boy, the newspapers carried a comic-strip character called "Casper Milquetoast." Casper was weak, ineffective, painfully shy, and retiring. He was the kind of person who would knock at a door and hope no one would answer because he did not want to confront people. That is the popular caricature of meekness.

Nor is this distortion absent from common perceptions of Christ. The passage that says, "Take my yoke upon you and learn of me, for I am meek and lowly in heart" is too often linked with "Gentle Jesus, meek and mild, You were once a little child." Thus some religionists portray the Lord Jesus with a thin, ascetic face and a passive demeanor, doing nothing bold or decisive.

But that is not what the New Testament records. The one who said, "I am meek and lowly in heart" was the same one who strode into the Temple with the scourge, overturned the money changers' tables, and declared that these people were not to make his Father's house a place of thievery.

Why can such a one be characterized as meek? Because the biblical definition of meekness is radically different from the popular conception. Meekness in Scripture is an uncompromising subordination to the will of God so that his will is primary in the life of the individual. Thus the Lord Jesus could say, "I do always those things that please my Father."

Similarly, Moses could say, in effect, that he wanted to do everything so as to please God. That explains the behavior of this meek man as he came down from the mountain: "He took the calf which they had made, and burnt it in the fire, and ground it to powder, and scattered it upon the water, and made the children of Israel drink it" (Exodus 32:21). What a dramatic scene that must have been, with group after group bending down to drink, some protesting, but all obeying, as Moses stood there with stern face and burning eye.

Next he dealt with his brother, Aaron, who had been left in charge. Interestingly enough Aaron's response was to try to put the blame on the people. "Let not the anger of my lord burn; they are set on mischief, for they said unto me, Make us gods, which shall go before us; as for this Moses, the man that brought us up out of the land of Egypt, we know not what is become of him. And I said unto them, Whosoever hath any gold, let them break it off. So they gave it to me, I cast it into the fire, and there came out this calf."

I can imagine Moses saying, "Aaron, are you telling me that this engraved calf *happened* to come out of the fire?" As usual, a lame excuse was worse than none at all. Moses was fully justified in rebuking his brother. Aaron had permitted himself to be manipulated by circumstance and public opinion. That is the opposite of biblical meekness.

Put yourself into this situation. What if your congregation or your people or those under your authority completely turned away from what you knew was right, and your assistant joined together with them? Some would be tempted, in the interest of harmony, to overlook the whole thing. But this is really not an option to the biblically meek leader.

Furthermore, Moses was also obliged to deal forthrightly with the people. He called to him those in the group who apparently had not followed the majority, and ordered them to impose judgment on the flagrantly disobedient. As a result, three thousand people died because Moses, a meek person, believed that a vital principle was involved. The sovereignty of God had been challenged. For that reason, the same man who pleaded with God on the mountain not to destroy the people, now made the people drink the polluted water, as well as executed those who were the most flagrant in their behavior.

Recognize the leadership principle involved here. A leader is not out to win a popularity contest but to uphold the ideals he is obliged in integrity to maintain. If this involves the rebuke or the punishment of subordinates, then such action must be taken for the sake of the cause to which the leader is committed.

Do you know what too often happens at this point? A reaction sets in when people are involved in inflicting judgment on others, unless they have the extraordinary quality that Moses had. Their sensitivities become dulled and they get a perverse pleasure out of watching people squirm. Thus we should recognize that there is something about inflicting punishment that can harden us to the point where we become less than our best.

Just the opposite was true of Moses. He was magnificent as he went to the Lord and said (in Exodus 32:31, 32): "This people have sinned a great sin, and have made them gods of gold. Yet now, if thou wilt forgive their sin—; and if not, blot me, I pray thee, out of thy book which thou hast written."

Do you see the consistency here? On the mountain, Moses would not accept the proposition that the people be destroyed so that God could make of him a great nation. He also refused to countenance evil, knowing that it too was inconsistent with the will and purpose of God. But he did not allow his feelings to cause him to reject Aaron and the people. Rather he offered to be judged in their place if only God would spare them.

This reminds me of the Apostle Paul's statement that he could wish himself accursed for his kinsmen, his brethren according to the flesh. These for whom he yearned were the very people who hounded him from city to city and who tried repeatedly to have him killed. Yet he was able to say that for them he would forfeit his eternal destiny.

So the mark of the Christian leader is a meekness that is bold and decisive in standing for God's Word and God's reputation. It is also a meekness sufficiently detached to feel no sense of vindictiveness or personal ambition. And it is a willingness to be set aside if only the Lord's cause can be advanced.

It would be natural to suppose that Israel, in a chastened mood, would have learned their lesson, so that in the future they would have accepted Moses without questioning his leadership. Unfortunately, this was not the case. From this we should learn that even though something has been done for a group that indicates concern for them, they will not necessarily accept their leader from then on. Indeed, the reaction in time may be quite the opposite.

On one occasion the head of a Christian organization called in one of his subordinates to explain why he was not at that time being given a permanent appointment. He candidly discussed a number of factors that resulted in this decision. A few weeks later a colleague came to see the leader. He said the employee in question had asked him to come and find out what the real reasons were for the decision in his case. In response the leader pointed out that if the truth had not been told the first time, there was no assurance it would be told now.

Rather than being bothered by others' tendency toward mistrust, the Christian leader should recognize that even Christian groups will expect him to reaccredit his leadership, just as Israel expected Moses to do. They were God's chosen people and a very select group. Yet they expected that this man who had literally put his life on the line for them and had given them such devoted and creative leadership, should regularly reaccredit his leadership.

The Christian leader must also recognize that God will hold him to a high standard of accountability. An illustration of this in Moses' life is described in Numbers 20. The first part of the chapter recounts the crisis that provoked Moses' reaction. "There was no water for the congregation: and they gathered themselves together against Moses and against Aaron. And the people strove with Moses, and spoke, saying, Would God that we had died when our brethren died before the Lord! Why have you brought up the congregation of the Lord into this wilderness, that we and our cattle should die there? And have you made us to come up out of Egypt, to bring us unto this evil place? It is no place of seed, or of figs, or of vines, or of pomegranates; neither is there any water to drink."

This kind of reproach was calculated to lacerate feelings, especially in light of the blessings and the miracles that Israel had already experienced. In reaction, Moses permitted his exasperation to get the better of him. He struck the rock rather than speaking to it as God had commanded. While God was gracious to provide the needed water anyway, he also held his servant accountable for his disobedience, as explained in verse 12: "And the Lord spake unto Moses and Aaron, Because ye believed me not, to sanctify me in the eyes of the children of Israel, therefore ye shall not bring this congregation into the land which I have given them."

As Moses described this experience later, he disclosed how he asked the Lord if he could at least cross the Jordan to see the Promised Land. He said, "I besought the Lord at that time, saying, O Lord God, thou hast begun to shew thy servant thy greatness, and thy mighty hand: for what God is there in heaven or in earth, that can do according to thy works, and according to thy might? I pray thee, let me go over, and see the good land that is beyond Jordan, that goodly mountain, and

Lebanon, But the Lord was angry with me for your sakes, and would not hear me: and the Lord said unto me, Let it suffice thee; speak no more unto me of this matter" (Deuteronomy 3:23-26).

One might ask whether a great leader who had led the people through the wilderness to the edge of the Promised Land might not be excused for his momentary lapse of self-control. One might remind the Lord that Moses had done many good things and had been so consistent throughout so much of his life that he deserved to have this one incident overlooked. As I have thought along these lines I have been reminded of this Scripture: "To whom much is given, of him shall much be required" (Luke 12:48). Moses knew that in spite of the provocation of the people, he was to go out and speak to the rock. He knew also that in losing his temper he stepped out of his position as a meek person. Instead of an uncompromising acceptance of the will and purpose of God, he acted to elevate himself and vent his displeasure on the people.

This should be a warning to all of us in positions of Christian leadership. The more we grow in the Lord, and the more we enjoy the privileges he gives us, and the more we rejoice in our opportunities to know God's will and purpose, the more accountable we are to do what we know is right. It is no excuse that the people provoked us.

Furthermore, if we complain that the pressures are more than we can bear, and in so doing imply that the Lord cannot or will not help us, he may take us at our word and relieve us of our responsibilities.

That was Elijah's experience, described in 1 Kings 19. After being threatened by Jezebel, Elijah fled into the wilderness and said, "It is enough; now, O Lord, take away my life; for I am not better than my fathers." In response, the Lord nourished him and then confronted him with the wind, the earthquake, the fire, and finally the still small voice. In reply to the Lord's question, Elijah voiced what seems to be a complaint that, in spite of his faithfulness to the Lord, he had been left alone and threatened. To this the Lord replied by instructing him to anoint Elisha to be a prophet in his place.

I have learned a lesson from this. If we let our emotions get out of control or if we complain to the Lord that we cannot take the pressure any longer, he is liable to take us at our word and instruct us to hand over our assignment to another. So sometimes I have told the Lord, "O God, I am in agony and do not know whether I can stand it or not, but I am not saying that I want to be relieved of my responsibilities. I know that you are able and willing to help me."

Despite the Lord's judgment of Moses for his failure, a New Testament reference highlights the goodness of the Lord toward Moses above and beyond what might have been expected. The incident is in Matthew 17: "And after six days Jesus taketh Peter, James, and John his brother, and bringeth them up into a high mountain apart, and was transfigured before them: and his face did shine as the sun, and his raiment was white as the light, and behold, there appeared unto them, Moses and Elijah talking with him."

At the time of the event, Jesus and the three disciples were in the Promised Land. Thus even though God did not let Moses go into the Promised Land with his people, he graciously let him enter the Promised Land on the Mount of Transfiguration that day, to talk with the Lord Jesus and with Elijah. In speculation on my part, I imagine that Moses might have told the Lord how much he appreciated all this, after he had lost his temper and dishonored the Lord's name, so that he deserved his punishment to stay on the other side of Jordan. Yet he had the privilege of entering the land and even having a conversation with God's incarnate Son.

Some conclusions may be drawn from this incident. If our shortcomings necessarily and properly bring God's punishment, he still is merciful and gracious. When we see his entire plan for us we will be moved by an overwhelming sense of gratitude. We will find that God is not only fair but also generous and merciful, far beyond what we deserve.

This incident also says something to us about the use or misuses of whatever strength we have. Sometimes a person's greatest strength can also be his greatest problem. I have known missionaries, for example, who remained on a difficult mission field only because they had the greatest of determination. But when they came home, they appeared extraordinarily arbitrary and stubborn. Insisting that whatever they believed was right, they refused to make changes even where others had insights on which they might well have based certain beneficial changes. They had to have that kind of single-mindedness on the mission field or they would have broken and run; but at home their strength could become a problem because the very thing that held them to their position also made them inflexible.

In Moses' case his tendency to become aroused was constructive when he came down from the mountain and judged the people; but it was misused at the waters of Meribah.

This should give us something to think about. We should analyze ourselves to see where our strengths may also be our weaknesses. If we are very open to suggestions and willing to listen to various viewpoints, do we lack decisiveness? If we are very decisive, are we prone to be impulsive and act before we think? This is what we can learn from Moses. Strengths of arousement and action can be misused. We need a certain amount of self-examination to discover how to maintain our strengths and not let them become weaknesses. As we do so we can improve the quality of our leadership.

CHAPTER TEN
RATIONALIZING
1 Samuel 15:1-35

SAUL WAS ISRAEL'S FIRST KING. His reign provides a number of important insights into the subject of leadership. From his experience we may learn what to avoid as well as what to accept and practice.

While he did not seek the monarchy, Saul was an impressive man with kingly credentials. In chapters 9 and 10 of 1 Samuel we see a description of Saul that tells us something about his qualifications. For one thing, he was tall and handsome. Ronald Knox has an interesting translation of 1 Samuel 9:2: "a fine figure of a man, none finer in Israel." Quite possibly he looked like one of our rugged, handsome athletes—a man's man. Despite this, he was a modest man. He accepted the fact that his family was not well known or prominent in Israel. And when they tried to find him to make him king, he was hidden among the baggage.

From chapter 10 we know that God endowed him supernaturally as well, for Scripture says that God gave him "another heart." Furthermore, he was privileged to have associates who also were gifted by God. Verse 26 says: "There went with him a band of men, whose hearts God had touched."

Early in his reign, Saul showed uncommon charity. Some

had objected to his becoming king; yet when he had experienced his first triumph and was urged to be vindictive, his reply was: "There shall not a man be put to death this day: for today the Lord hath brought salvation in Israel." Without question, then, Saul had substantial natural and supernatural endowments. This makes all the more significant the record of his reign.

Several key factors determined Saul's course of action and his ultimate downfall. These should be instructive to all who have the responsibilities of leadership. The first of these is described in 1 Samuel 13:8ff:

"And he [that is, Saul] tarried seven days, according to the set time that Samuel had appointed: but Samuel came not to Gilgal; and the people were scattered from him. And Saul said, Bring hither a burnt-offering to me, and peace-offerings. And he offered the burnt-offering. And it came to pass, that as soon as he had made an end of offering the burnt-offering, behold, Samuel came; and Saul went out to meet him, that he might bless him. And Samuel said, What hast thou done? And Saul said, Because I saw that the people were scattered from me, that thou camest not in the days appointed, that the Philistines gathered themselves together at Michmash; Therefore said I, The Philistines will come down upon me to Gilgal, and I have not made supplication unto the Lord: I forced myself therefore, and offered a burnt-offering."

We may deduce from this account that on the basis of expediency Saul was willing to disobey a biblical principle. He knew that only the priests of the Lord were to offer sacrifices. He was of the tribe of Benjamin, and not a priest. Yet in the crisis in which he found himself, he was willing to violate a law of God. He told himself that the circumstances justified the violation.

Today we call such rationalizing *situation ethics*. Those who espouse this position argue that while a biblical commandment may apply in a majority of cases, there are exceptions. For example, sexual immorality is usually wrong, they say, but if it results in personal fulfillment, then it may be justified.

Nor is this type of rationalization absent from evangelicalism. Some years ago a man spoke at Wheaton in one of our gatherings. It was at a time of year when relatively few people attended. Some time later, a public relations agency that was doing some work for him wrote and asked for a photograph of the occasion at which he had spoken, in order to use the picture in some publicity materials. We sent the photograph. A few days later the agency returned the photograph with a notation that it was unacceptable. They asked that we send a picture of the auditorium filled with people. We declined. Their intent was to build the image of their client, apparently assuming that he would be more used of God if the public got the impression that he spoke to an overflow crowd. Apparently truthfulness seemed less important than the reputation of their client. I suspect that the man himself was not aware of what his agency was doing; but what happened illustrates the tendency even among Christians to base actions on manipulative factors rather than on principles.

What must have astonished Saul was that immediately after he offered the sacrifice, here came Samuel. God frequently tests us that way. If we are tempted to set aside a commandment of God to do something that is expedient, the lesson is clear—don't do it.

My wife and I make frequent trips to Chicago's O'Hare Airport. Sometimes it seems as if some little creature goes before us turning the traffic lights red all the way to the field. This seems to happen particularly when we have left later than we should have. The temptation is to go through on red if no one is coming.

We could rationalize this by arguing that we must get there before takeoff. Often when we have resisted this temptation but driven under pressure, we arrive only to find that the flight has been delayed. Then I can almost hear the Lord saying, "I knew it all the time. Why did you get so upset?" So if I had gone through red lights and broken the law and justified it by saying that I had to get on that airplane—and then found it was late, I would certainly conclude that being governed by the circumstance of the moment was unjustified.

That is what happened to Saul. In another few minutes, Samuel came. How much better it would have been had Saul refused to be controlled by circumstances and instead had held fast to what he knew was right.

The second factor is illustrated by an incident described in the fourteenth chapter of 1 Samuel. Jonathan and his armor bearer attacked the enemy and defeated them. As a result, all the people were gathered together to the battle. At that time, Saul issued a command: "Cursed be the man who eateth any food until evening, that I may be avenged on mine enemies. So none of the people tasted any food" (1 Samuel 14:24).

But Jonathan, not having heard the commandment, saw some honey, put the end of his staff into it, and ate some of it. As a result, he gained some quick energy and felt built up again. But someone told his father. This precipitated a crisis. Saul told Jonathan he would have to die because he had broken his commandment. Outraged by what seemed an unfair judgment, the rest of the people prevented Saul from carrying out his threat. The effect of this showdown became evident later.

An important lesson grows from this event. Occasionally a leader will issue an order or give a directive that is unreasonable, even denying his subordinates what they need to do their job. In desperation, people may then take things into their own hands. That is what happened here: "The people flew upon the spoil, and took sheep, and oxen, and calves, and slew them on the ground: and the people did eat them with the blood" (verse 32). Israel knew it was a sin to eat the blood, but they were too hungry to care.

Be assured that if you establish regulations which deny people what is necessary for them to do their work, they will find a way to meet their need, though they may do it in the wrong way.

I know of organizations that pay their employees less than they should—scarcely a living wage. Their employees find it necessary to take supplementary jobs in order to meet their obligations. Then sometimes when they are asked why they were not on hand at a given time, they try to evade the issue by saying that they just were not available. The fact is that they were occupied elsewhere. Not being paid enough, they find another way to meet their need. But the method used contradicts their commitment to the organization. How much better it is to pay a living wage and have people giving full measure, than to have them tired, preoccupied, or sometimes unavailable.

Some organizations impose restrictions on employees' criticisms, pay little heed to their suggestions, or provide little opportunity to talk things out. You know what happens. The criticism is there. The talk goes on. But opinions are expressed in the wrong places, usually producing distrust, alienation, and disloyalty. The man at the top may think everything is fine until conditions have reached a crisis. How much better to provide legitimate ways for expression of opinions.

We can learn from Saul's mistake of issuing an arbitrary and unreasonable command which caused the people to disobey God by eating blood. If we profit from his mistake, we may avoid the problem that developed out of his error and contributed to his being rejected by the Lord.

A third factor came from Saul's incomplete obedience when he was commanded to destroy the Amalekites and all that they had. The Scripture describes Samuel's confrontation of Saul this way: "And when Samuel rose early to meet Saul in the morning, it was told Samuel, saying, Saul came to Carmel, and, behold, he set him up a place, and is gone about, and passed on, and gone down to Gilgal. And Samuel came to Saul: and Saul said unto him, Blessed be thou of the Lord: I have performed the commandment of the Lord. And Samuel said, What meaneth then this bleating of the sheep in mine ears, and the lowing of the oxen which I hear?"

Disobedience will make fools out of us. What Saul said was so obviously untrue. How possibly could he have said that he followed the commandment of the Lord? Yet when he was disobedient, he became fearful, and to defend himself, said things that were ridiculous.

Now let us return to the biblical narrative: "Saul said, They have brought them from the Amalekites: for the people spared the best of the sheep and of the oxen to sacrifice unto the Lord thy God." Notice the reasoning here. The justification for disobeying God was that they obtained materials with which to worship the Lord. It would be akin to stealing money to make up a tithe.

What was Samuel's response? "Then Samuel said unto Saul, Stay, and I will tell thee what the Lord hath said to me this night. And he said unto him, Say on. And Samuel said, When you were little in your own sight, were you not made the head of the tribes of Israel, and the Lord anointed thee king over Israel? And the Lord sent thee on a journey, and said, Go and utterly destroy the sinners the Amalekites, and fight against them until they be consumed. Why then didst thou not obey the voice of the Lord, but didst fly upon the spoil, and didst evil in the sight of the Lord?" Notice Saul's reply to that question and Samuel's rejoinder. "Saul said unto Samuel, Yea, I have obeyed the voice of the Lord, and have gone the way which the Lord sent me, and have brought Agag the king of Amalek, and have utterly destroyed the Amalekites, but the people took of the spoil, sheep and oxen, the chief of the things which should have been utterly destroyed, to sacrifice unto the Lord thy God in Gilgal. And Samuel said, Hath the Lord as great delight in burnt offerings and sacrifices, as in obeying the voice of the Lord? Behold, to obey is better than sacrifice, and to hearken than the fat of rams. For rebellion is as the sin of witchcraft, and stubbornness is as iniquity and idolatry. Because thou hast rejected the word of the Lord, he hath also rejected thee from being king."

I don't think Samuel said this harshly. I think he spoke with a trembling voice and with tears in his eyes. In any event, Saul at last acknowledged his sin. He confessed to Samuel, "I have sinned; for I have transgressed the commandment of the Lord, and thy words: because I feared the people and obeyed their voice."

Relate this incident to the one in the previous chapter. There, because of an unjustified restriction, the people took things into their own hands and refused to let Saul execute Jonathan. I suspect that they determined that the next time they went out to battle and there was spoil to take, they were not going to get caught short again. In case the king made another arbitrary decision not to take spoil, they were going to get as much as they could before he changed his mind.

This reminds me of something in my Navy days. When we went ashore, we would go over the gangway and onto the dock, and we would run as fast as we could for the gate. We had a reason for our haste. Sometimes when we had been all set to go ashore, and had asked permission to leave the ship, we had been told to load ammunition or to do some other task. Then we would think about all those who had already left while we had to start operating a hoist or loading ammunition. You can imagine what we were thinking. Next time we plan to go ashore, we'll get on that dock and run for that gate. Then we'll be away before any announcement to remain on board to load ammunition.

I am not proud of the way we ran for the gate. But it was a natural reaction to being kept aboard when everybody else had gone ashore. And I think this was the attitude of the people under Saul. Since they got no spoil the previous time, now they were going to take all they could get. The result was that the king, who had been overly arbitrary, lost the confidence of his subjects and eventually could not control them.

In a sense Saul was right when he said the people did it. No longer could he get them to obey him. Yet he was the king. He was accountable for what they did. Anyone in a responsible position may permit subordinates to act independently, but the leader is still held accountable. That is the price of leadership.

The last incident we shall consider in this connection is in chapter 28. Taken with the others, this chapter shows a pattern of deterioration that I believe is not only chronological but also logical. First came expediency in place of principle. Then, in reaction to that expediency, an arbitrariness that went to the other extreme. Then a loss of confidence and control that resulted in putting unjustified blame on subordinates.

All of this culminates in Saul's effort to call up Samuel in order to tell him what was to happen, for the Lord no longer spoke to Saul. He was experiencing the truth of Psalm 66: "If I regard iniquity in my heart, the Lord will not hear me." So he was a leader who not only was discredited among his people, but also was unable to receive the guidance and wisdom and enablement he needed from the Lord.

That is the sobering lesson to be learned from the life of this pathetic leader. Once principle is abandoned in favor of expediency, followed by over-arbitrary action, people begin to think of you as quixotic and incapable of consistency. Then there is the mistake of trying to shift the blame to others as if your decisions were simply the result of consensus. The combination of disobedience and abdication results in a loss of God's fellowship and consequently of God's wisdom and power. In such a state it is difficult both emotionally and spiritually to act decisively. The result is frustration and futility.

Dr. Douglas McGregor, after six years as president of Ohio's Antioch College, commented: "I believed a leader could operate successfully as a kind of adviser . . . avoid being a boss. Unconsciously, I suspect, I hoped to duck the unpleasant necessity of making difficult decisions, of taking the responsibility for one course of action among many uncertain alternatives, of making mistakes and taking the consequences . . . I couldn't have been more wrong. It took a couple of years, but I finally began to realize that a leader cannot avoid the exercise of authority any more than he can avoid responsibility for what happens to his organization." This observation was in a section of Dr. McGregor's address that he entitled, "The Boss Must Be Boss." Saul provides a vivid illustration of one who needed to learn what Dr. McGregor found by experience to be true.

From the life of Saul we can learn to base our leadership upon principle and to characterize our leadership by consistency and balance. That, I submit, will merit the respect and the cooperation of your subordinates.

CHAPTER ELEVEN
MORE THAN WISDOM
2 Chronicles 1:1-13

THE CHRISTIAN LEADER NEEDS WISDOM. The complexities and the perplexities of his calling are such that we sometimes say he needs the wisdom of Solomon. But a consideration of Solomon's life makes plain that he needs more than wisdom if his performance is to please God.

Solomon had much in his favor when he began his public role as king of Israel. One factor was the blessing of God upon him from his birth, as we see in 2 Samuel 12:24: "And the Lord loved him. And he sent by the hand of Nathan the prophet; and he called his name Jedidiah, because of the Lord." The name *Jedidiah* means "beloved of the Lord." In that very name Solomon had the assurance that God loved him.

Remember too that the choice of Solomon from among David's children to be king was of the Lord. We know this from the statement in 1 Chronicles 29:1: "Furthermore David the king said unto all the congregation, Solomon my son, whom alone God hath chosen, is yet young and tender." While we have no elaboration of this, it seems clear that David was persuaded God had led him to designate Solomon as his successor. This he made explicit in his statement to the congregation.

Solomon also had the benefit of his father's intercessory

prayer. The essence of the prayer is in 1 Chronicles 29:13: "And give unto Solomon my son a perfect heart, to keep thy commandments, thy testimonies, and thy statutes, and to do all these things, and to build the palace, for which I have made provision." The fuller text of this prayer is in Psalm 72, where we cannot help being impressed by the petitions David made to God on behalf of his son. He asked for acceptance, blessing, power, and influence.

I know something of this kind of blessing from personal experience, for I had godly parents. One of the reasons I have missed my mother during the years that she has been with the Lord, is because she was so faithful in her intercessory ministry for me. I believe that I was often preserved morally and spiritually as well as physically because Mother stood in the gap, so to speak, to pray for her son. I thank the Lord for this. The same may be said for my father. During one of his visits he told me that he prays for me every day. That is a tremendous resource, far more significant than we may realize.

While we may not be able to demonstrate a direct cause and effect relationship, it is probable that some of the difficulties Solomon encountered may have occurred because David had died and was no longer an intercessor for his son. Yet such ministry is not limited to parents. If you know someone who is prominent and successful, pray for that person. And urge others to pray for you. This cannot help but make a difference in undergirding a leader's ministry. Of course Solomon himself was certainly personally accountable, but perhaps he might have done better if he could have continued to receive the support which David provided during his lifetime.

I am aware of the criticism of David that he did not adequately discipline Solomon. Perhaps there is a basis for that criticism. But 1 Chronicles 28 suggests a concern which was not limited to prayer. This may be seen particularly in verse 9 and following, where David charges Solomon explicitly:

"Solomon my son, know thou the God of thy father, and serve him with a perfect heart and with a willing mind: for the Lord searcheth all hearts, and understandeth all the imaginations of the thoughts; if thou seek him, he will be found of thee; but if thou forsake him, he will cast thee off forever. Take heed now; for the Lord hath chosen thee to build an house for the sanctuary: be strong, and do it."

Thus David publicly exhorted Solomon to keep in mind that serving the Lord would bring blessing while disobeying him would bring judgment.

Furthermore, when Solomon came to the throne, he received a special bestowment from the Lord. Notice 1 Chronicles 29:25: "And the Lord magnified Solomon exceedingly in the sight of all Israel, and bestowed upon him such royal majesty as had not been on any king before him in Israel." This happens today as well as in Solomon's time. When the Lord calls a person to a position of leadership, that individual is in a sense magnified in the sight of the people so that he may properly exercise the responsibilities of leadership. This is one of God's gracious bestowments.

Then in the first chapter of 2 Chronicles we have the well-known encounter between the Lord and Solomon. Verse 7 says, "In that night did God appear unto Solomon, and said unto him, Ask what I shall give thee." The remarkable thing here is that Solomon did not come to the Lord, but instead the Lord appeared to Solomon and invited him to ask. In our day we do not need visions in the night, because we know from New Testament teachings that we are invited to come and ask. But at that time it was a gracious and wonderful thing for the Lord to invite Solomon to ask what he wanted.

I suggest that Solomon's reply issued from his background and experience. The exhortations and the prayers had prepared his mind and heart to respond by asking for wisdom.

How generous is our Lord's response! "Wisdom and knowledge are granted unto thee; and I will give thee riches, and wealth, and honor, such as none of the kings have had that have been before thee, neither shall there any after thee have the like" (2 Chronicles 1:12).

Keep in mind the special preparation and the specific provisions made for Solomon, because we also may have particular enduements from the Lord for our tasks. For example, those of us in positions of leadership certainly need wisdom, and we have this promise in James 1:5, 6: "If any of you lack wisdom, let him ask of God that giveth to all men liberally and upbraideth not and it shall be given him. But let him ask in faith, nothing wavering." Like Solomon we can receive wisdom by asking.

With this by way of context, let us consider two major tests that came into Solomon's life, both of which are prominent in our culture today. The reference for the first of these is in the closing part of 1 Kings 6 and the opening part of chapter 7. The challenge was whether Solomon was able to handle wealth. God had said he would have wealth, and he was probably the richest man in the world at that time.

With this in mind, notice an interesting contrast. In 1 Kings 6:37 we read, "In the fourth year was the foundation of the house of the Lord laid, in the month Zif: and in the eleventh year, in the month Bul, which is the eighth month, was the house finished throughout all the parts of it, and according to all the fashion of it. So was he seven years in building it." But in chapter 7 we read: "But Solomon was building his own house thirteen years, and he finished all his house."

I recognize that David had made preparation for the building of the Lord's house in that he had accumulated materials in abundance. Thus Solomon would be able to build without delay. We might surmise, therefore, that this reduced the building time somewhat. Even so, there was a substantial difference between the seven years to build the Lord's house and the thirteen years to build Solomon's. To me this suggests that while Solomon was faithful in building the Temple of the Lord and establishing it as a place of worship, he was more interested in the building of his own house. The attraction of material things had so penetrated Solomon's consciousness that his priorities were out of order.

Here I can anticipate what you may be thinking. You may ask, "How can we determine what is an appropriate commitment of money to personal things or to goods and services that we need, as compared to what we should commit to the work of the Lord?" Without seeking to evade the question, I believe there is no simple, uncomplicated formula for this. I commend for your reading two passages in the New Testament which do not deal specifically with material things as such, but with matters of discretion in which there is no explicit moral or ethical pronouncement. The passages are Romans 14 and 1 Corinthians 8. These passages discuss the question of eating meat offered to idols, and of keeping a particular day. It is not the specifics of these two chapters that I have in mind here, but the principle that I believe underlies both of them. That principle is that each individual must make an examined decision whether to eat meat or not, and whether to keep the day or not. Similarly, we must make examined decisions about whether to commit financial resources in one way or another.

In the 1960s some young people declared, often with great heat, that if a man had more than one suit jacket, he was out of the will of God. They also made a practice of quoting the last part of Acts 4, which says that the church had all things common. Even today, groups of Christians have agreed to pool their resources and live very simply. I respect their decision but do not believe that every Christian is necessarily called to such a manner of life.

My reason for saying this is found in the opening portion of Acts 5. In the account of Ananias and Sapphira, Peter told that pair that while they had the land, it was their own, and when they sold it, the proceeds were to be used at their discretion. Now if there was no discretion but rather an absolute that everyone *had* to sell his land and give all to the church, Peter would not have spoken that way. Instead, there was opportunity for personal judgment. Christians could keep their land if the Lord led them to do so, or they could sell it. What was determinative was God's sovereign purpose. Once they sold it, they could give all the proceeds or a part. That was between them and the Lord. It was not an absolute imposed on the entire church.

So with respect to things material, let us not insist that every Christian fit into exactly the same mold. On the other hand, let us not fall prey to "keeping up with the Joneses." If they buy a new automobile, must we buy one? If they make an addition to the house, must we? If they own a boat and a house in the country, must we? If so, then we are caught in a tide of steadily rising expectations. Rather let us make an examined decision based upon whether an expenditure will enable us better to perform our ministry. If so, then I would say, at the risk of being misunderstood, relax and make the expenditure.

One might for example question spending on air-conditioning. Is it just for personal comfort, or is it in some instances an aid to a significantly better fulfillment of one's God-given role in life? Another might bring up the question of clothing and personal appearance. Should ministers of the gospel, for example, dress in blue jeans? That is not really the question. The issue is whether what we wear is conducive to effectiveness with the group to which we are ministering. Sometimes young people ask why it is not appropriate to wear what they call "grubbies" for virtually every occasion. My answer is that when our appearance calls attention to ourselves rather than to the message that our ministry is to deliver, it is out of place.

When I am ranching in West Texas, I do not wear a suit and tie on the range. Instead, I wear blue jeans, boots, and a western hat. My appearance depends on the circumstances. Out on the ranch, I look like a rancher; before a group of business executives I look like a college president. I believe an expenditure for a well-fitting suit is justified. It is preferable to wearing some outlandish costume that calls undue attention to me. I recognize that some Christians justify their dress as a sign of poverty and obedience. Yet even this can sometimes make the wearer an exhibitionist who enjoys calling attention to himself. Whatever your decision in this matter, let it be an examined one.

Scripture offers no indication that Solomon used his extraordinary wisdom to ascertain whether or not he needed all the opulence with which he surrounded himself. To me, it appears that he had gone far beyond the point of necessity even for a king. He could not justify what was really in excess.

Let us learn from Solomon's experience. We should examine the way our budgets are built. We should ask whether we really do need this or that item. If before the Lord we are persuaded that we should or should not have a particular building or vehicle or item of clothing, other Christians should be able to respect our integrity because they sense that we have made an examined decision before the Lord. What is essential is that we be open to his leading, whatever it may be. If we feel at rest about it after taking the matter to him, then I believe it is inappropriate for others to say that we are out of the will of God. On the other hand, if our administrative style manifests that we have thought little about it but simply had the money and spent it, then we deserve to be rebuked. I believe Solomon had the money and spent it without asking the Lord about it. This got him into trouble.

The other major test that came into Solomon's life is also present in our American culture. The description of Solomon's experience is in this passage, from 1 Kings 11: "But king Solomon loved many foreign women, in addition to the daughter of Pharaoh, women of the Moabites, Ammonites, Edomites, Zidonians, and Hittites; of the nations concerning which the Lord said unto the children of Israel, Ye shall not go in to them, neither shall they come in unto you: for surely they will turn away your heart after their gods: Solomon clung to these in love. He had seven hundred wives, princesses, and three hundred concubines: and his wives turned away his heart. For it came to pass, when Solomon was old, that his wives turned away his heart after other gods: and his heart was not perfect with the Lord his God as was the heart of David his father. For Solomon went after Ashtoreth the goddess of the Zidonians, and after Milcom the abomination of the Ammonites. And Solomon did evil in the sight of the Lord, and went not fully after the Lord, as did David his father. Then did Solomon build an high place for Chemosh, the abomination of Moab, in the hill that is before Jerusalem, and for Molech, the abomination of the children of Ammon. And likewise did he for all his foreign wives, which burnt incense and sacrificed to their gods."

Keep in mind that this is the action of the wisest man who ever lived, the man who understood clearly the text and meaning of Holy Scripture and who in writing the Proverbs pointed out the pitfalls of sexual lust. Obviously, his wisdom was not enough. This reminds me of an incident that occurred when my wife and I were first married and on our way to San Pedro, California, where my ship was in dry dock. We were traveling by train, in a sleeping car of the type that had curtains to provide privacy for the upper and lower berths. The berths were made by flattening out the seats and lowering an upper wall section. The curtains then formed inner walls along the center aisle.

After my wife and I had gone to bed we heard a conversation through the curtain. The porter was talking to a young lady. She had come down the aisle to the place just opposite us, where a young military officer had his berth. She was about to enter that berth with him when the porter said, "Miss, you know this is wrong. Please don't do it." I shall always remember her response. She said, "I know it's wrong, but I am going to do it anyway." And she did.

Solomon too knew that his sexual life was wrong, but lust had so gripped him that he simply was not going to turn aside from it. Sexual license had become a preoccupation with him and he was not about to give it up. In so doing he ignored clear warnings and exhortations.

God himself warned Solomon about the consequences of disobedience, in 1 Kings 9: "When Solomon had finished the building of the house of the Lord . . . the Lord apeared to him a second time . . . and the Lord spoke to him. If thou wilt walk before me, as David thy father walked, in integrity of heart, and in uprightness, to do according to all that I have commanded thee, and wilt keep my statutes and my judgments: Then will I establish the throne of thy kingdom upon Israel forever, as I promised to David. But if ye shall at all turn from following me, or your children, and will not keep my commandments and my statutes which I have set before you, but go and serve other gods, and worship them: then will I cut off Israel out of the land which I have given them: and this house, which I have hallowed for my name, will I cast out of my sight; and Israel shall be a proverb and a byword among all people: . . . because they forsook the Lord, their God, who brought forth their fathers out of the land of Egypt . . . "

A later remonstrance is recorded in 1 Kings 11: "The Lord said unto Solomon, Forasmuch as this is done by thee, and thou hast not kept my covenant and my statutes, which I have commanded thee, I will surely tear the kingdom away from thee, and will give it to thy servant. And the Lord stirred up an adversary unto Solomon, Hadad, the Edomite: he was of the king's seed in Edom. And God stirred up another adversary, Rezon the son of Eliadah, which fled before his lord. And Jeroboam the son of Nebat . . . even lifted up his hand against the king."

Notice how persistently God acted to dissuade Solomon from his course of self-gratification and inordinate lust. He warned him, rebuked him, and allowed three adversaries to oppose him. He told him that he was going to lose the kingdom, and that Israel was going to be disgraced and rejected because of his action. So the wisest man who ever lived could not plead that he was unaware of these things.

Solomon stands as an illustration of what happens when lust controls an individual. It radically distorts his judgment and his perspective. In effect, his whole being is inverted so that the visceral dominates the cerebral. This is why the prophet Nehemiah could remind Israel (13:26): "Did not Solomon king of Israel sin by these things? . . . even him did outlandish women cause to sin."

For Christian leaders the point is clear. One way Satan will try to destroy the leader's testimony (and that of those associated with him) is through illicit sex. It is important that the leader not start down this path in his mind through sexual fantasies induced by magazines, photographs, or conversation. All such must be decisively set aside so that the leader does not capitulate in his mind. If he does, he will capitulate in his behavior also. Sometimes people accept the fallacy that it is the socially deprived and the ignorant who are sexually promiscuous. That is not true. Like Solomon, unfortunately, the highly educated and the ones who know the consequences also go down the same sordid road.

A key passage in the New Testament provides a vivid contrast to this. The Scripture I have in mind is in the last part of 1 Corinthians 1 and the opening part of chapter 2. We have said that wisdom is not enough. But for those of us in Christ, wisdom has a much more comprehensive connotation. This may be seen from the passage as translated in the New International Version: "It is because of him that you are in Christ Jesus, who has become for us wisdom from God, that is, our righteousness, holiness, and redemption."

The distinction is most important. Solomon had extraordinary wisdom in knowing what were the right decisions to make. He possessed unusual mental ability. But in Christ Jesus, New Testament wisdom is more than that. It now includes righteousness, holiness, and redemption. Such wisdom is supernaturally mediated to us in our Savior. And such wisdom gives us not only sensitivity but also ability to live lives of righteousness and holiness and redemption. This is truly liberating wisdom.

This passage also gives us an illustration of its point. If you were asked to identify the most brilliant and intelligent man in the New Testament, your choice would probably be the Apostle Paul. Besides being naturally gifted, Paul had an excellent education. That is why his self-appraisal is so significant. He said: "I, brethren, when I came to you, came not with excellency of speech or of wisdom, declaring unto you the testimony of God. For I determined not to know anything among you, except Jesus Christ, and him crucified. And I was with you in weakness, and in fear, and in much trembling. And my speech and my preaching were not with enticing words of man's wisdom, but in demonstration of the Spirit and of power: that your faith should not stand in the wisdom of men, but in the power of God."

The great evangelist D. L. Moody was accused of murdering the King's English. The fact that he may have done so does not justify the practice, but his ministry illustrates for us the distinction between an eloquent, finely honed sermon that is devoid of spiritual power, and one characterized by the dynamic of the Holy Spirit. The one celebrates man's wisdom; the other elevates God's power.

Years ago in New England we heard about a young woman who said she was no longer a Christian. She had made a profession of faith under the ministry of one of the most brilliant men I have ever known—a man who had not only an outstanding mind, but also a singular dedication to scholarship. As she listened to him, she was impressed with the logic and comprehensiveness of his presentation, as we all were at the time. Then the minister was called of God to another part of the country. When he left, the young woman's faith collapsed. She was a Christian as long as her teacher was there. Once he was gone, she was no longer interested in being a Christian.

The Apostle Paul knew of that possibility. So do most

preachers. One of the greatest temptations they have is to minister in the energy of the flesh. It can be done. The notorious case of the man known as Marjoe bears this out. For years he was able to get people to come to the front of packed auditoriums in response to his invitation even though, if you can believe him now, it was all a sham.

When I was a student at the University of Chicago, I took a course in American religious movements. The professor told of clinical studies of meetings in which everything had been carefully orchestrated. At the end of each sermon there was a death-bed tale or other tear-jerking story. Then as soft music played in the background, people were influenced by an emotional appeal to come down to the front. The point was that it did not matter whether an evangelical was preaching or not. By using mass psychology people could be emotionally aroused so that they would come to the front in some sort of commitment.

Admittedly such manipulation is possible. But are the results durable? How much better to have our witness characterized by the wisdom that God has given us, so that it is not our wisdom but the Lord who is glorified. Then people will respond genuinely and lastingly, because of the authenticity of what we had to say about Jesus Christ, not because of some clever salesmanship.

Does this rule out apologetics, or vigorous study? No, but these efforts must be rooted in 1 Corinthians 1:30 and then expressed with great sensitivity and care as the Apostle Paul did, in order that those to whom we minister will not have their faith resting upon our brilliance and wisdom, but in the power of God.

CHAPTER TWELVE
HANDLING SUCCESS
2 Chronicles 32:20-33

ONE OF THE MOST FORMIDABLE tests a leader must face is success. This is especially true when his record of faithfulness in itself is most commendable. King Hezekiah was confronted with just such a challenge. He had been unusually faithful in his reign as king over God's people, but when he trusted in himself rather than in God, he learned just how inadequate such misplaced trust can be.

Hezekiah's background was quite different from that of Solomon. We see a description of Hezekiah's father in 2 Kings 16:2: "Twenty years old was Ahaz when he began to reign, and reigned sixteen years in Jerusalem, and did not that which was right in the sight of the Lord his God, like David his father. But he walked in the way of the kings of Israel, yea, and made his son to pass through the fire, according to the abominations of the nations, whom the Lord cast out from before the children of Israel. And he sacrificed and burnt incense in the high places, and on the hills and under every green tree."

To have that kind of father is a great liability. Yet it is a mistake to think that the only way to be a success is to have a proper background. Hezekiah is a dramatic exception to that notion. Such exceptions do not invalidate parents' responsibility to provide a good background, but they do suggest the children's personal accountability as they grow up in any family.

Had he lived in our day, Hezekiah might very well have been perceived as having only a marginal chance of becoming a leader of integrity. Many would assume that he would not possess high moral and ethical qualities because his parental influence was so bad. Fortunately, this was not the case. This suggests, therefore, that a true leader will develop personal ideals and convictions rather than excuse himself for moral and ethical deviations because of a poor background. Hezekiah stands as an inspiring example of one who rose above his parental influence to become a man of God.

When he came to the throne at the age of twenty-five, Hezekiah immediately instituted a series of reforms. One of the most important of these was the reestablishment of the Temple worship which had fallen into disuse. Hezekiah was able to get things done so that his people could worship in the Temple again. His reason for doing this was that when the Temple was in disuse, people resorted to alternate means of worship, resulting in a religious syncretism—a mixing of contradictory faiths.

Some years ago my father visited in Central America and brought back a photograph of a church. Immediately in front of the church, a fire was burning. My father learned that the religious people who came to that community years before had built the church to counteract the pagan rites of the people in their worship of the Fire God. So a church was constructed in the same location where these rites were held. But instead of making a clear distinction between the two forms of religion, the people developed a syncretism. They would come to the entrance of the church and build a fire to worship the Fire God. Then they would proceed into the church in an effort to obtain the best of both worlds.

To avoid this kind of thing in his day, Hezekiah recognized it would be necessary to establish the kind of worship that had been commanded by the Lord God. He realized that the

Temple would be the focal point for this. At the same time it would be necessary to abolish all other forms of worship.

Secondly, he reestablished the Passover. This suggests something that is of concern to me—an emphasis that is becoming evident in evangelical circles. A great deal of stress is being placed upon personal relationships. In fact, for some, the concept of salvation is little more than the experience of a dynamic encounter. Furthermore, the functions of the gathered church tend increasingly to reflect current cultural ideas. As a result, some of the major events that brought the church to where it is today are suspect because they are viewed as embarrassing or anachronistic.

As a convinced Protestant, I believe that October 31st is an appropriate time to talk about the Reformation. My purpose is not to generate hostility toward the church out of which the Reformation came, but to recognize that certain important truths were recovered at that time—truths that are central to what we believe today: Scripture alone, faith alone, and direct access to the presence of the Lord. These things are worth an annual emphasis. I have discovered, however, a reluctance to highlight the Reformation or to include it on the Christian calendar. With this in mind I suggest that our Protestant and evangelical congregations can benefit from some special reminder on Reformation Sunday. We should rejoice in the acts of God that are part of our heritage.

When Hezekiah reestablished the Passover, he restored a ceremony that reminded God's people of one of the great events connected with their emancipation. We all need such reminders. You recall the condemnation in our Lord's statement in the Revelation: "I have somewhat against you because you have left your first love." Perhaps that occurred because the Ephesian church had lost some of the sense of what Hezekiah sought to recover through the Passover—awareness of the deliverance from bondage and from Egypt into the liberty of the Promised Land.

While it is inappropriate to dwell constantly on the past, it is fitting periodically to reflect upon what we were before we came to Christ. Thus, Hezekiah, with a perspective that was scriptural and historical, summoned the people to celebrate the Passover, even asking those from beyond the borders of his kingdom to join with them in the remembrance at Jerusalem. And his effort proved successful.

But after his accomplishments, based on commendable convictions, Hezekiah in time came to face what I would call the problem of success. From his experience we can learn that a leader with an outstanding record and biblical convictions may still be vulnerable to the temptations that success brings.

One of the major triumphs in Hezekiah's life was his people's deliverance from Sennacherib. The enemy had come to the gates of the city. The Assyrian king's representative, Rab-shakeh, threatened the Jews on the wall, using their own language. Realizing the critical nature of the situation, Hezekiah committed the entire matter to the Lord, acknowledging his need of divine help and praying that in it all God would be glorified. In response, the Lord delivered Hezekiah and his people, giving them a tremendous victory. No doubt Hezekiah was thereafter perceived as a man of extraordinary faith, for one hundred and eighty-five thousand of the enemy were killed by the intervention of God.

Some may conclude from this that a nation need only trust in God and the enemies of the country will be defeated. Such a conclusion is overdrawn. Yet there is no doubt in my mind that some military actions show the providential workings of God.

The Battle of Midway is a twentieth-century instance. The timing of the deployment of the Japanese submarine and the search plane, along with the change in orders aboard the Japanese carrier to load the planes with different armament, provided the United States forces with circumstances that resulted in a major Naval victory. In retrospect, some analysts have concluded that if the series of events had not actually occurred, the whole sequence would be classified as too unlikely for fiction—something that simply could not have happened. Yet it did indeed take place.

So we must recognize the intervening hand of God in human affairs, but we must also recognize that if God were to deliver his people in that way as a general practice, then much of the Old Testament must be called into question. Time and again God did *not* choose to act in that way, but rather commanded his people to go out and wage war. So while we indeed must entrust ourselves to a sovereign God to preserve us as a nation, as Hezekiah did, we should not make a broad generalization that invalidates other portions of Scripture. Indeed, some who believe that God will act apart from the use of armed forces do not leave social justice, for example, solely to his divine intervention. On the contrary, they stress personal involvement to effect needed change.

Let us consider now the supreme crisis in Hezekiah's life. A description of this is in 2 Kings 20: "In those days was Hezekiah sick unto death. And the prophet Isaiah the son of Amoz came to him, and said unto him, Thus saith the Lord, Set thine house in order; for thou shalt die, and not live. Then he turned his face to the wall, and prayed unto the Lord, saying, I beseech thee, O Lord, remember now how I have walked before thee in truth and with a perfect heart, and have done that which is good in thy sight. And Hezekiah wept very much.

"And it came to pass, before Isaiah was gone out into the middle court, that the word of the Lord came to him, saying, Turn again, and tell Hezekiah the captain of my people, Thus saith the Lord, the God of David thy father, I have heard thy prayer, I have seen thy tears: behold, I will heal thee: on the third day thou shalt go up into the house of the Lord. And I will add unto thy days fifteen years; and I will deliver thee and this city out of the hand of the king of Assyria: I will defend this city for mine own sake, and for my servant David's sake.

"And Isaiah said, Take a lump of figs. And they took and

laid it on the boil, and he recovered. And Hezekiah said unto Isaiah, What shall be the sign that the Lord will heal me, and that I shall go up into the house of the Lord on the third day? And Isaiah said, This sign shall thou have of the Lord, that the Lord will do the thing that he hath spoken: shall the shadow go forward ten degrees, or go back ten degrees? And Hezekiah answered, It is a light thing for the shadow to go down ten degrees: nay, but let the shadow return backward ten degrees. And Isaiah the prophet cried unto the Lord: and he brought the shadow ten degrees backward, by which it had gone down in the dial of Ahaz."

If I had been Hezekiah at thirty-nine years of age, I suspect I too would have had some deep feelings. I might have said, "Well, Lord, since life begins at forty, isn't my probable death a bit premature?" No doubt that is why Hezekiah rehearsed to the Lord all that he had done as described in Isaiah 38. In response, the Lord told the prophet to advise Hezekiah that fifteen years would be added to his life.

This importunate request of Hezekiah reminds me of a verse which some years ago struck me with great force. It is Psalm 106:15. I recognize that this Psalm is talking about the children of Israel rather than an individual, but I think the principle here applies individually as well as collectively. The verse reads: "He gave them their request; but sent leanness into their soul."

Sometimes I have heard people say in their prayers, "God, you have got to do this." And where they have insisted that their request be granted, there are times when that is the way things turned out. The apparent conclusion is that this is the way to approach God. To get results is to insist upon having your request. But this verse of Scripture suggests that our insisted-upon results may not be favorable.

Others criticize the use of the phrase, "If it be God's will," as some kind of escape mechanism so that no matter what happens, it can be said that God had his way. Yet there is a sublime example in the use of "If it be your will" in prayer. In

Gethsemane Jesus prayed, "Oh, my Father, if it be possible, let this cup pass from me, nevertheless, not as I will, but as thou wilt." I am prepared to follow the example of our Lord Jesus. Otherwise, God may grant my request but send leanness into my soul.

Some couples have acknowledged that they were called of God to serve on the mission field, only to begin to think about things that we all consider significant. They wondered what would happen if they had children who would have to be separated from them to attend a mission school. They became concerned about their health. They questioned whether they could find a proper outlet for the abilities God had given them. So in effect they said to the Lord, "We insist that we stay home." And they did so. But now, in middle life, they experience an emptiness of life and a sense of futility. Now they wish they had not demanded their own way, but rather had been willing to accept the will and purpose of God for them.

The objection might be raised that this is all well and good when the issue has to do simply with one option or another in our ministry. But when one's life is at stake, it is only natural to plead with God to be able to live a little longer. But here the experience of Hezekiah is particularly instructive. He had been very successful in faith and action. Would he now continue to live to the glory of God if he were to live longer?"

The answer to that question may be seen in what occurs after Hezekiah was healed. As soon as he was restored to health, he had a change of attitude, described in 2 Chronicles 32:24 and following: "In those days Hezekiah was sick to the death, and prayed unto the Lord: and he spoke unto him and he gave him a sign. But Hezekiah rendered not again according to the benefit done unto him; for his heart was lifted up: therefore there was wrath upon him, and upon Judah and Jerusalem. Notwithstanding Hezekiah humbled himself."

In crying out and asking to be healed, Hezekiah thought only about saving his life. But God knew that when he was healed, rather than giving glory to God, he would become proud and boast that he was healed after being at the point of death, and that furthermore, he had been guaranteed fifteen more years of life.

This is not an easy matter to handle. If you or I knew that we were guaranteed fifteen more years to live, we might well reason that we had ample time to do this or that. The years would slip by swiftly while we procrastinated. Whether this was also Hezekiah's problem or not, it is clear that he could not handle the success and blessing that had been given him. God knew this and would have saved him from doing what later discredited him.

This attitude of pride showed in what he did when the emissaries came from Babylon to visit him. The account of this is in 2 Kings 20:12-21: "At that time Berodach-baladan, the son of Baladan, king of Babylon, sent letters and a present unto Hezekiah: for he had heard that Hezekiah had been sick. And Hezekiah hearkened unto them, and shewed them all the house of his precious things, the silver, and the gold, the spices, and the precious ointment, and all the house of his armour, and all that was found in his treasuries: there was nothing in his house, nor in all his dominion, that Hezekiah shewed them not. Then came Isaiah the prophet unto king Hezekiah, and said unto him, What said these men? and from whence came they unto thee? And Hezekiah said, They are come from a far country, even from Babylon. And he said, What have they seen in thine house? And Hezekiah answered, All the things that are in mine house have they seen: there is nothing among my treasures that I have not shewed them.

"And Isaiah said unto Hezekiah, Hear the word of the Lord. Behold, the days come, that all that is in thine house, and that which thy fathers have laid up in store unto this day, shall be carried into Babylon: nothing shall be left, saith the Lord. And some of thy sons that shall issue from thee, whom thou shalt beget, shall they take away: and they shall be eunuchs in the palace of the king of Babylon. Then said Hezekiah unto Isaiah, Good is the word of the Lord which thou hast spoken. And he said, Is it not good, if peace and truth be in my days? And the rest of the acts of Hezekiah, and all his might, and how he made a pool, and a conduit, and brought water into the city, are they not written in the book of the chronicles of the kings of Judah? And Hezekiah slept with his fathers, and Manasseh his son reigned in his stead."

We may infer from Hezekiah's later rebuke from Isaiah that he took pride in all of these things as if they were his own possessions, rather than what he held in stewardship for the Lord. God in his omniscience knew that Hezekiah, if he were spared, would not only glory in the act of healing rather than in the Healer, but also would become preoccupied with the wealth of his kingdom rather than with the Giver of all these things. Thus Hezekiah turned from the Blesser to the blessings.

If God has a time for us to die, we ought to acknowledge that he knows best even though it is natural for us to cling to life. This is not to suggest that we be presumptuous or refuse to used medical means or to be careful. It does mean, however, that we are to trust our sovereign Lord to do what is best.

Consider the experience of Paul Little, the Inter-Varsity Christian Fellowship worker who became so well loved on university campuses. His view of God's sovereignty over his life was included in his last article published in *Moody Monthly*. In that article he stated his conviction that God never makes any mistakes. Soon afterward, while he was driving north to Toronto, his car went out of control and this gifted man, whose ministry has been a blessing to thousands, was killed. We could argue that Paul should have been spared to help his wife and the children, and to continue his strategic ministry to young people. In bewilderment and almost in despair, we are tempted to ask God, "Why did you take Paul Little?" Ruth Graham eloquently expressed this feeling in the poem she wrote when she got the news of Paul's Homegoing. None of us knows the answer to this question now, except that God does not make any mistakes.

In my combat experience during World War Two, I saw the providential hand of God at work time after time. On several occasions the ship in which I served could have been sunk. I recall one incident particularly. When a naval vessel is at sea, an officer who is called the officer of the deck is stationed on the bridge. During his watch he is in charge of the ship by direction of the commanding officer. One night, even though I was qualified as an officer of the deck, I was standing watch, from midnight to 4:00 A.M., in the combat information center. This center received and disseminated information from the various radars and radios. A signal came over the tactical radio network from the Admiral's staff that the formation was to change course. We were in a formation with four carriers plus several cruisers and destroyers. I deciphered the signal, which was in code, and knew that we were to come to a particular course and speed at a certain time.

But when I called the bridge on the intercommunications system and reported my understanding of the radio message, the officer of the deck replied that I was mistaken. That was surprising, but since he was the officer of the deck, I could not overrule him. Then came the command to execute the signal. The rest of the formation came to the new course while we stayed on our original heading. Then I called the bridge to report that the carrier was at 500 yards. Soon it was too close to be seen on the radar. When no acknowledgment came from the bridge, I told the men on watch with me that in just a minute the bow of the carrier would come through the bulkhead and cut the ship in two.

Our ship's doctor was sleeping in a cabin on the main deck. He had opened the portholes because of the heat. Something caused him to wake up. As he looked out of his porthole, he saw the enormous shape of the carrier just a few yards from him and rushed into the combat information center to find out what was happening.

We found out later what took place. The officer of the deck on the carrier had brought his ship around and, as was the practice, looked through his field glasses. Even though the ships were blacked out, a trained observer could see their shapes in the darkness. He thought he saw a ship about to cross his bow, so he checked with his own combat information center. Then he realized we had not changed course. So he ordered his engine room to reverse engines, and gave the command to close the watertight doors. Since it takes a ship the size of a carrier some distance to stop, it came to within a few yards of our side.

Eventually we came to the new course and all was well. I think that incident demonstrated the providential care of almighty God. If the carrier had not stopped, I would not be here today.

From this and other experiences I believe that the circumstances of life are not matters of fate but the providence of God. Only he can keep us alive. When the time comes that we are to die, he will permit this to happen. In so doing he may very well be sparing us or others from something that we could not know about at the time, and would not know about until we are in the Lord's presence.

This was also true for Hezekiah. Only in eternity would he realize what could have been avoided had he died at thirty-nine. In 2 Chronicles 33:1 we read, "Manasseh was twelve years old when he began to reign, and he reigned fifty and five years in Jerusalem." When was Manasseh born? He was born during the fifteen additional years that God gave Hezekiah. Scripture repeatedly makes the point that Manasseh was one of the most wicked and brutal kings ever to reign over Judah. The biblical account says that he filled Jerusalem with the blood of his victims. God knew that if Hezekiah lived longer, it would not only be for his own hurt, but also for the oppression of the people of God because of Manasseh's persecution, bloodshed, and tyranny. If Hezekiah had died when God said he should, he would never have had Manasseh as a son.

When we demand that God must do it our way, we demonstrate that our perspective does not fit with the biblical view of life, of death, and of eternity. We see the outcome for Hezekiah in 2 Chronicles 32:31: "Howbeit in the business of the ambassadors of the princes of Babylon, who sent unto him to enquire of the wonder that was done in the land, God left him, to test him, that he might know all that was in his heart." When we say to God that he must do what we want, we in effect are saying that our judgment is better than his. In response God may very well withdraw his informing, protecting, restraining ministry, and leave us to ourselves.

That was the underlying reason for Hezekiah's pride and indiscretion in his disclosures to the visitors from Babylon. God left him to himself. No doubt it is because he is aware of this principle that Dr. Billy Graham repeatedly says that if God were to withdraw his hand, his lips would turn to clay. That is not merely a statement for the press. That is the profound conviction of a man who has learned this biblical lesson and is saying in effect: "Lord, don't leave me to myself, because I already know what is in my heart, and I don't trust my own judgment."

Hezekiah is a compelling illustration of one who had strong convictions, great faith, and unusual experiences of deliverance, but was not prepared to trust God for the ultimate destiny of his life. He apparently became too attached to success and to status and to all the good things God had given him.

His experience provides also another lesson for those in Christian leadership. It is this: God may not ask us to give up our lives, but he may test us just as dramatically as he did Hezekiah by asking us to come to the place where, in effect, it would be the same as if we had died. That is, we would no more have our assignment, our resources, our authority, or our subordinates.

If all of these were to be withdrawn, would we still trust the Lord? Or would we say that the price is too high, and ask to stay in our present situation? The Christian leader may have no idea why he is being asked to withdraw from all the excitement, the blessing, and the challenge of his work, as if God had told him he was going to die. But he must understand that if God asks this of him, it is so that he might do the Lord's will.

Let us ask ourselves whether we serve the Lord merely because he blesses us or because he is Lord. And if he is Lord, can we not trust him to do the very best for his glory and for our benefit? Indeed we can. And as we do so, we can deal with success because our commitment is not to the blessings but to the Benefactor.

CHAPTER THIRTEEN
CONSISTENT
GROWTH
Matthew 16:13-27

PERSONAL GROWTH IS ESSENTIAL to good leadership. Far from thinking he has attained, the effective leader is continually seeking to learn from his experiences and become even more proficient in his work. The Apostle Peter is an example of this kind of growth. His mistakes tended to be public and dramatic, but the saving feature of his career was his desire to improve.

One of Peter's major problems was his tendency to act first and think later. An instance of this is found in Matthew 14, beginning with verse 25: "And in the fourth watch of the night Jesus went unto them, walking on the sea. And when the disciples saw him walking on the sea, they were troubled, saying, It is a ghost; and they cried out for fear. But straightway Jesus spake unto them, saying, Be of good cheer; it is I; be not afraid. And Peter answered him and said, Lord, if it be thou, bid me come unto thee on the water. And he said, Come. And when Peter was come down out of the boat he walked on the water, to go to Jesus. But when he saw the wind boisterous, he was afraid; and beginning to sink, he cried, saying, Lord, save me. And immediately Jesus stretched forth his hand, and caught him and said unto him, O thou of little faith, wherefore didst thou doubt? And when they were come into the boat, the wind ceased. Then they that were in the boat came and worshipped him, saying, Of a truth thou art the Son of God."

This experience summarizes Peter's manner of life, and it highlights the necessity of growth. The same pattern can be seen in the other instances we shall consider. Repeatedly Peter responded in immediate but unthinking enthusiasm to the challenge of the moment and then had second thoughts as the realities of the situation became clear to him. Fortunately, by one means or another he was corrected and restored. This caused him to grow in his awareness of what it meant to serve the Lord.

With this as a general proposition, let us look at some other pertinent illustrations that show Peter's progression toward maturity. Then we should notice also some insights in his epistles that were written just before his martyrdom, reflecting a spiritually mature perspective on the matter of commitment to the Lord.

The first instance is in Matthew 16:13-26: "When Jesus came into the borders of Caesarea Philippi, he asked his disciples, saying, Who do men say that I the Son of man am? And they said, Some say that thou art John the Baptist; some, Elijah; and others, Jeremiah or one of the prophets. He saith unto them, But who say ye that I am? And Simon Peter answered and said, Thou art the Christ, the Son of the living God.

"And Jesus answered and said unto him, Blessed art thou, Simon Bar-jona; for flesh and blood hath not revealed it unto thee, but my Father which is in heaven. And I say unto thee, That thou art Peter, and upon this rock I will build my church; and the gates of hell shall not prevail against it. And I will give unto thee the keys of the kingdom of heaven: and whatsoever thou shall bind on earth shall be bound in heaven; and whatsover thou shalt loose on earth shall be loosed in heaven. Then charged he his disciples that they should tell no man that he was Jesus the Christ. From that time forth began Jesus to shew unto his disciples, how that he must go unto Jerusalem, and suffer many things of the elders and chief priests and scribes, and be killed, and be raised again the third day.

"Then Peter took him, and began to rebuke him, saying, Be it far from thee, Lord: this shall not be unto thee. But he turned, and said unto Peter, Get thee behind me, Satan: thou art an offence unto me: for thou savourest not the things that be of God, but those that be of men. Then said Jesus unto his disciples, If any man will come after me, let him deny himself, and take up his cross and follow me. For whosoever will save his life, shall lose it: and whosoever will lose his life for my sake shall find it. For what is a man profited, if he shall gain the whole world, and lose his own soul? or what shall a man give in exchange for his soul?"

This narrative describes an event that followed two significant happenings, both of which highlighted ways of knowing or understanding. I believe these were included in the biblical text so that they might stand in contrast to the essential nature of Peter's confession.

In the opening part of the chapter our Lord was confronted by the Pharisees and the Sadducees, and he answered them this way: "When it is evening you say it will be fair weather for the sky is red, and in the morning it will be foul weather today for the sky is red and overcast; O ye hypocrites, ye can discern the face of the sky; but can ye not discern the signs of the times?"

What kind of knowledge was our Lord describing? It was knowledge gained by observation—by what we could call descriptive or discursive knowledge. In effect, Jesus was saying that these people were capable of predicting the weather by observation but were not demonstrating that they could discern the significance of events—something they should have been able to do from their knowledge of Holy Scripture. Their perspective was obviously limited. Descriptive knowledge can be part of the divine disclosure as is true of the revelation of God in nature. Romans 1 tells us this can be seen from the creation and thus men are accountable because of it; but it is a limited disclosure.

Then in verse 6 and following, Jesus tells his disciples,

"Beware of the leaven of the Pharisees and of the Sadducees. And they reasoned among themselves, saying, It is because we have taken no bread. Which when Jesus perceived, he said unto them, O ye of little faith, why reason ye among yourselves, because ye have brought no bread? Do ye not yet understand, neither remember the five loaves of the five thousand, and how many baskets ye took up? How is it that ye do not understand that I spake not to you concerning bread, but that you should beware of the leaven of the Pharisees and of the Sadducees? Then understood they that he bade them not to beware of the leaven of bread, but of the doctrine of the Pharisees and of the Sadducees."

That which the disciples did illustrates a second kind of knowledge. This is pondering something and then deducing a conclusion. When the disciples heard the Lord Jesus tell them to beware of the leaven, they remembered that they had forgotten to bring any bread. So they concluded that the Lord was indirectly reminding them of their oversight.

We might ask why it was that the disciples who saw the Lord feed five thousand on one occasion and four thousand on another could not have concluded that he was perfectly capable of supplying their need for bread as well. I see at least two reasons for their limited outlook. One is that they were not open to understand the implications of the miracles because their hearts were hardened (see Mark 6:52). That is, they were predisposed to reject the supernatural. The other is that human speculation is limited. Unaided by revelation, we cannot grasp a higher coherence apart from the informing ministry of God himself.

Thus, when the Lord told Peter that it was not flesh and blood but the Father in heaven who revealed the person of Christ to him, he was saying that such an insight did not come through discursive or speculative knowledge but through revelational knowledge. This implies that certain truths about the person of Christ or about eternity or about the nature of man can be known only by revelation. To be sure, these truths may be illustrated in nature. We may study man and be confirmed in our thinking that he is sinful because of his behavior, but apart from revelation we cannot explain how he got that way, or how he can be delivered from his condition.

We recognize that Peter was divinely ordained to receive this special revelation and to articulate it. This he did with enthusiasm but apparently without reflecting on what his confession meant. Otherwise, how could he by divine revelation confess Jesus as the Messiah, the Son of the living God, and so soon afterward rebuke him for saying as God's Son and the Christ, that he was to suffer and die?

One explanation for Peter's action is that he became proud about being the recipient of divine revelation. Having had this disclosure from God, he thought he was now competent to speak on any subject whatsoever.

I have found some Christians to be that way. Because they have an intensive knowledge in one field and have become expert in it, they conclude that they are authorities about almost everything else as well. Unfortunately, this does not follow. Nor does one experience indicate that all succeeding experiences are going to be the same. A degree of humility would spare them the dire results of such presumption.

Those of us in higher education struggle with this problem often. After having had unusual opportunities to study and to become expert, it is easy to take our expertise and elevate it to an unwarranted absoluteness. Just because as a Ph.D. I said something does not make it so. It is a tragic situation when an educated person is unwilling to apply the same rigorous investigative and evaluative procedures to other fields of knowledge that he applies within his own discipline. Unfortunately, those of us in higher education do not always do this. When I was an historian, I was very careful to look up the sources and have two or three references for every fact. Yet I found it easy when I heard a rumor to accept it without testing its validity. In such matters I was not employing the rigorous tests for truth that were standard procedure in my discipline.

Similarly, Peter should have concluded that even though he was the recipient of divine revelation, he was certainly not qualified to tell Jesus that he was mistaken.

Some earnest but misguided Christians tell us that some of the biblical writers were wrong. I tremble when I hear of this, because I think of the Lord's rebuke to Peter. The questioning of God's Word does the work of the enemy. Remember that the first time God's Word was questioned was in the Garden of Eden, when Satan remarked, "Yea, has God said?" That same question mark over the Word of God is present with us today as well. That is why we need to understand why Jesus turned to Peter and said, "Get thee behind me, Satan." He knew very well that the campaign which was begun in the Garden of Eden was being continued through the one who had just been commended as a vehicle of divine revelation.

This should give us pause because it suggests that those of us who know the Lord and who are his disciples might be tempted the same way. We need to be extraordinarily careful in coming to God's Word that we do not question its truthfulness. That opens the way for the enemy to come in and exploit the situation for his own ends.

The question remains, however, as to what motivated Peter to act as he did. I believe the tendency noted in Matthew 14 was present here as well. This was a concern for self-preservation. Notice that immediately after our Savior rebuked Peter, the Scripture says: "Jesus said to his disciples, If any man will come after me, let him deny himself, take up his cross, and follow me. For what is the advantage if a man gains the whole world and loses his own soul?"

I am convinced that when the Apostle Peter heard Jesus saying that he was going to go to Jerusalem and suffer many things from the elders and chief priests and scribes, and be killed, he became so preoccupied with this that he did not hear the Lord also say that he would be raised the third day.

Some may wonder whether such selective deafness is really possible. I assure you that it is, for it has happened to me. I have been listening to a sermon when I begin to think about what the minister has just been saying while he continues to preach. Then I come back to where he is in his message but I have missed the intervening sequence because of preoccupation with what he said earlier. In the interval I was not listening.

Similarly I believe Peter was not listening when the Lord spoke about being raised the third day. This was because when he heard that his Lord was going to be taken and persecuted by wicked hands and be crucified, he began wondering what was going to happen to him. And so he rebuked the Lord in an effort to change his mind. Knowing that Peter did not want to suffer and die, the Lord Jesus spoke to the issue by saying that if any man would come after him, he must deny himself and take up his cross and follow him. Even more specifically, he confronted Peter with the question as to what it would profit him if he were to gain the whole world, and lose his own soul.

So the exhortation about discipleship and its cost is integrally related to our Savior's statement about his going to the cross, and to Peter's anxiety about what that would mean for him personally. This parallels the incident in which Peter walked on the water. As he looked at the circumstances, all of his confidence in the Lord and his power was displaced by an anxiety for his own safety. As a result he began to sink. He needed the help of the Lord to save him. In this instance as well, he began to sink into unbelief because of a concern for his own welfare. He needed the Savior's strong and realistic word to overcome his doubts and restore his faith.

To all who acknowledge their discipleship to Jesus Christ, this message is timeless. It is only natural to be threatened when facing the prospect of tribulation and persecution. But for the disciple, escape from these is not an option. Instead, there must be a resolute decision to follow Christ at all costs, recognizing that the eternal rewards are both glorious and enduring.

The second illustration from Peter's experience is his denial of our Lord. The account of this is in Matthew 26. To understand the denial as consistent with the pattern we have been considering, we need first of all to consider the content. This begins in verse 31: "Then saith Jesus unto them, All ye shall be offended because of me this night: for it is written, I will smite the Shepherd, and the sheep of the flock shall be scattered abroad. But after I am risen again, I will go before you into Galilee. Peter answered and said unto him, Though all men shall be offended because of thee, yet will I never be offended. Jesus said unto him, Verily I say unto thee, That this night, before the cock crow, thou shalt deny me thrice. Peter said unto him, Though I should die with thee, yet will I not deny thee."

Here again the pattern is evident. There is an enthusiastic pledge of allegiance, so to speak. This time, however, the Lord spoke directly to Peter before he was confronted with the circumstance. In effect, he said that he understood Peter's problem and knew that when he got into a threatening circumstance he would deny his Lord. It was almost as if Jesus was asking Peter to remember what had happened to him before.

In that context the Lord was telling him that on the basis of his divine insight all of the disciples, including Peter, would be offended because of him that night. Thus he clearly pointed out Peter's problem. Despite that, Peter was not ready to accept the possibility of his ever denying Jesus. His attitude seemed to be that though he may have failed his Lord in the past, now he had enough self-confidence and trust in his convictions never to deny him again.

See how patient the Lord is with his disciple. When he walked on the water and then began to sink, the Savior reminded him that he had but little faith. Thus he should have more faith in him and less concern for circumstances. Then, when Peter had the divine revelation about Christ's person, the Lord had to remind him that this truth, rather than his own well-being, must be central. Now Jesus once again urges Peter to recognize that his natural tendency will be to flee because of what is about to happen. Yet Peter was still not able to recognize his problem. Once again he was presumptuous enough to reject the Lord's prediction.

The fulfillment of this prediction is described in the closing part of the chapter, beginning at verse 69: "Now Peter sat without in the palace and a damsel came unto him, saying, Thou also wast with Jesus of Galilee. But he denied before them all, saying, I know not what thou sayest. And when he was gone out into the porch, another maid saw him, and said unto them that were there, This fellow was also with Jesus of Nazareth. And again he denied with an oath, I do not know the man. And after a while came unto him they that stood by, and said to Peter, Surely thou also art one of them; for thy speech betrayeth thee. Then began he to curse and to swear, saying, I know not the man. And immediately the cock crowed. And Peter remembered the word of Jesus which said unto him, Before the cock crow, thou shalt deny me thrice. And he went out, and wept bitterly."

I consider this a turning point in the growth of this man. It is a crisis that others also have experienced in their Christian walk. When we trust in ourselves apart from God's grace and power, there will be occasions when we will realize with painful awareness the complete poverty of our own resources to meet the particular crisis or issue that has come into our lives. In Peter's case, it was a misplaced confidence in himself that got him into the crisis in which he acted to protect himself, despite the commitments he had made. All of this combined to show him just how needy he was.

Incidentally, for years I was troubled when I read that Peter denied Jesus with an oath and began to curse and to swear, for I projected a twentieth-century concept of cursing and swearing and oaths into this situation. Now I believe that what Peter did was to use the affirmations that for a Jew were binding. That makes his actions even more pathetic. In our parlance, he was standing up, putting one hand on the Bible, and raising the other hand to say, "I solemnly swear to tell the truth, the whole truth, and nothing but the truth, so help me, God. I do not know that man."

When the cock crowed and Peter remembered Jesus' words, the realization of what he had done struck him with great force. No doubt he recalled that he not only had declared his intentions privately in the presence of the disciples, but also had publicly affirmed, as if he were an honorable man whose word was to be trusted, that he did not even know his Lord. He had completely contradicted what he had told Jesus earlier. Thus, God graciously permitted him to be brought to the point where with great clarity he could see what his problem really was.

Thank God, the Lord did not leave him there in a state of painful awareness. He provided an opportunity for Peter's restoration to fellowship and to meaningful service. Now that Peter was prepared to grow in his faith and to seek to apply it in practice, the method the Savior used is described in the well-known passage in John 21: "So when they had dined, Jesus saith to Simon Peter, Simon, son of Jonas, lovest thou me more than these? [using the word for divine love] And he saith unto him, Yea, Lord: thou knowest that I love thee [using the word for human love and affection]. He saith unto him, Feed my lambs. He saith to him again the second time, Simon, son of Jonas, lovest thou me? He said unto him, Yea, Lord: thou knowest that I love thee. He saith unto him, Feed my sheep. He saith unto him the third time, Simon, son of Jonas, lovest thou me? Peter was grieved because he said unto him the third time, Lovest thou me? [That is, do you even have an affection for me?] And he said unto him, Lord, thou knowest all things: thou knowest that I love thee. Jesus saith unto him, Feed my sheep."

Now notice what immediately follows: "Verily, verily, I say unto thee, When thou wast young, thou girdest thyself, and walkedst whither thou wouldest: but when thou shalt be old, thou shall stretch forth thy hands, and another shall gird thee, and carry thee whither thou wouldest not. This spoke he, signifying by what death he should glorify God. And when he had spoken this, he saith unto him, Follow me."

In this way the Lord addressed himself directly to the major issue in Peter's life. He had permitted Peter to get himself into a circumstance in which he denied the Lord three times. Then he graciously questioned Peter to give him opportunity for realistic but heartfelt reaffirmation of his commitment. But with the commissioning to feed the lambs and tend the sheep, the Lord immediately brought up the issue of self-preservation. He told Peter that his concern about jeopardy in serving Christ was actually well-founded. When he was older he would die a martyr's death. In light of that, since he had just told the Lord that he loved him, he was issued the command, "Follow me."

There is drama here. From Peter's past experiences, no doubt memories crowded in upon him. He probably recalled walking on the water and then being afraid for his own safety because he was not looking at the Lord but at the circumstances. He remembered hearing Jesus say he was going to be taken and crucified and how he feared for his own safety. He called to mind the Lord's statement that the disciples, including himself, would be scattered. He recalled his objection to that prediction and then his three-times denial.

I suspect that all this came into his consciousness at this point, and yet there was also evidence of growth. Peter now had come to the point of a realistic assessment of himself. No doubt he remembered the Lord's word as recorded in Matthew 16, that to be a disciple he would have to deny himself and take up his cross. Before the crucifixion, that might well have been an abstract thought. Now it was a reality. From afar off he had seen his Savior stretched out upon the cross. He heard the curses of the crowd and their mocking and jeering. In his mind's eye he could see blood dripping from the Savior's body. Surely this must have come into his mind when the Lord told him that others would take him where he did not want to go, signifying the kind of death he was to die.

The tradition is that Peter was crucified upside down at his own request because he did not want to be crucified in the same posture as his Savior. If this is true, it suggests that Peter here faced realistically the fact that to serve Jesus Christ and to follow him would involve the losing of his life in a brutal and cruel way.

In all of this the Lord was doing what he did in dealing with the rich young ruler—and what he will do with us as well. He will test us at the point of our vulnerability, at that point most calculated to interfere with our devotion to him. The rich young ruler went away sorrowful, having great possessions. Some have concluded therefore that it is wrong to have wealth. That was not the issue. Rather it happened to be the key factor in the life of this young man. For Peter it was physical self-preservation. For one of us it might be our reputation, our family, or our special capabilities. Whatever it is, the Lord will challenge us at the point where there is the possibility that this particular factor will interfere with our unconditional commitment to him.

Such a crisis experience, however, does not necessarily guarantee that we will consistently apply our commitment to the circumstances or events of the future. To insure consistency and growth requires the ongoing ministry of the Lord in our lives. Frequently this is mediated to us through fellow members of the body of Christ.

The second chapter of Galatians includes the account of how one of Peter's brothers in the faith assumed the role that Jesus had during his incarnate ministry in dealing with Peter. The Apostle Paul describes the situation this way: "And when James, Peter and John, who seemed to be pillars, perceived the grace that was given unto me, they gave to me and Barnabas the right hands of fellowship; that we should go unto the Gentiles, and they unto the circumcision. Only they would

165

that we should remember the poor; the same which I also was diligent to do. But when Peter was come to Antioch, I withstood him to his face, because he was to be blamed. For before certain men came from James, he did eat with the Gentiles: but when they were come, he withdrew and separated himself, fearing them who were of the circumcision. And the other Jews dissembled likewise with him; insomuch that Barnabas also was carried away with their false pretense. But when I saw that they walked not uprightly according to the truth of the Gospel, I said unto Peter before them all, If thou, being a Jew, livest after the manner of the Gentiles, and not as do the Jews, why compellest thou the Gentiles to live as do the Jews?" Then in the remainder of the chapter he summarized his conversation with Peter.

The fact that Paul's rebuke was necessary was all the more remarkable because of what had happened to Peter as described in Acts 10. In preparation for the message from Cornelius, who was a Gentile, Peter had the vision of a sheet let down from heaven with all kinds of creatures on it. Peter was hungry and heard a voice telling him to kill these and eat them. Interestingly, Peter's familiar tendency to question the Lord showed itself even then. "Not so, Lord, for I have never eaten anything that is common or unclean." To this the voice replied that what God had cleansed, he was not to call common. For emphasis the experience was repeated three times.

I can sympathize with Peter because in my own experience I have had difficulty on occasion putting a propositional truth into action. In the late 1960s we saw changes on campus, not only in attitude but also in the appearance of some of our students. I then held (and still hold) some convictions about men having long hair. I believe it is inappropriate and biblically unjustified. Our student personnel staff urged, however, that we permit a degree of liberty in this matter.

We had some young men on campus whose hair was longer than I thought it should have been. They also began to dress in a manner more like the counter-culture. And I despised the counter-culture because to me it represented unpatriotic draft-resisters, flag-burners and such like. When I read of their acts as they rioted and demonstrated, my blood pressure rose because I remembered fighting for the country they despised. Though I had fought for all citizens to have the liberty to disagree, I resented the way the counter-culture went about disagreeing.

One day I was scheduled to speak in chapel. Just before the service, we gathered for prayer to ask the Lord's blessing. As we were about to pray, in walked a young man who had a beard and long hair, was wearing a sash around his waist, and had sandals on. As I looked at him, I was sorry he had come in. Worse yet, he sat down right beside me. When we went to prayer, I did not enter into the praying with a very good attitude. Then the young man began to pray, and his prayer went something like this: "Dear Lord, you know how much I admire Dr. Armerding, how I appreciate his walk with you. I am grateful for what a man of God he is, and how he loves you and loves your people. Lord, bless him today. Give him liberty in the Holy Spirit and make him a real blessing to all of us in the student body. Help us to have open hearts to hear what he has to say, and may we just do what you want us to do."

As I walked down the steps to go into the chapel, the Lord spoke to me about my attitude. After giving my message, I asked the young man to come to the platform. Later I learned that one of the students turned to another and remarked that I was probably about to dismiss the young man from school as an example to the rest of the students. Thus everyone, including the young man, was surprised when I put my arms around him and embraced him as a brother in Christ. That broke up the chapel service. Students stood and applauded; they cried and embraced each other. The reaction was unprecedented, and under God, seemed to change the mood on campus to one of greater love and acceptance of one another.

I learned later that the young man in question had adopted his appearance in order to be able to reach some of his generation who were alienated. Whether or not this was the case, I needed to learn not to reject someone whom God had cleansed. This does not mean that I now approve of the counter-culture or of the appearance of those in it or of those who look like they are in it. But I believe that if God has accepted another believer, I should do so as well. I should not reject him simply because of his style of life.

Fortunately, Peter was open to the Lord's instruction in this matter, even though it meant readjusting his manner of life after years of doing things differently. Thus, he responded when he was invited to the household of Cornelius, and he was candid enough to share his experience with them. Then he saw the Lord work in a supernatural way, confirming the leading he had been given, as the Holy Spirit came on the Gentiles.

But now in spite of this meaningful experience that was later endorsed by the church leaders in Jerusalem, a problem began to arise in Peter's mind. He reflected upon the fact that his status with his Jewish brethren might be jeopardized by his associating with Christians who were Gentiles. So the expediency of the moment prompted him to withdraw from having fellowship with the Gentiles so as not to offend his Jewish brethren.

To confront Peter, the Apostle Paul was God's instrument to remind him of what he knew very well but was not practicing. So Paul faced him with the fact that he, being a Jew, was living like the Gentiles. Hence, it was not right for him to expect the Gentile believers to live as the Jewish ones were persuaded they should. In saying this, Paul was summoning Peter to live out what he knew, by putting aside his anxieties about his status with his Jewish brethren, and by accepting in practice the unity of the body of Christ.

Here again, the Apostle Peter needed to grow. While he was no longer questioning whether his life was to be taken, he still had a problem about his relationship with others. Resolving this was a major advance in his growth in grace.

These incidents in Peter's experience correspond to the three major foes that we must face. In Matthew 16 it was Satan. In Matthew 26 it was Peter's concern for his flesh. In Galatians 2 it was his reputation with his world, the world of Jewish culture. The world, the flesh, and the devil still work together today to stunt the spiritual growth of the believer and to reduce his commitment to the Lordship of Jesus Christ.

Specific evidence for Peter's spiritual growth may be found in his epistles. The passages I shall mention are only representative. A careful reading of 1 and 2 Peter will make plain that in both of these epistles there are numerous references to the very things we have been discussing.

In 1 Peter 5:8 I believe the apostle refers to the experience recorded in Matthew 16. "Be sober, be vigilant; because your adversary the devil, as a roaring lion, walketh about, seeking whom he may devour: Whom resist stedfast in the faith, knowing that the same afflictions are accomplished in your brethren that are in this world." Manifestly, he had learned that Satan was a formidable foe but one who could be successfully resisted.

Then in chapter 2 of this same epistle, verse 11 says, "Dearly beloved, I beseech you as strangers and pilgrims, abstain from fleshly lusts which war against the soul; having your behavior honest among the Gentiles: that, whereas they speak against you as evil doers, they may by your good works, which they shall behold, glorify God in the day of visitation." From this statement it is obvious that Peter had learned not to give way to the flesh, even for self-preservation, so that he might be a good witness for his Savior.

Consider also his statement in 1 Peter 3, beginning with verse 13: "And who is he that will harm you, if ye be followers of that which is good? But and if ye suffer for righteousness' sake, happy are ye: and be not afraid of their terror, neither be troubled; but sanctify the Lord God in your hearts; and be ready always to give an answer to every man that asketh you a reason of the hope that is in you with meekness and fear; having a good conscience that, whereas they speak evil of you as of evildoers, they may be ashamed that falsely accuse your good manner of life in Christ. For it is better, if the will of God be so, that ye suffer for well doing, than for evil doing." Clearly, Peter had learned that faithfulness to the will of God was paramount, whether this was acceptable to those around him or not.

Thus in the closing years of his life he had come to some settled convictions. He would not allow Satan to take advantage of him, but would resist him steadfast in the faith. He would not allow his fleshly desires to get out of hand and cause his testimony to be compromised, but would keep his body disciplined under the sovereign power of the Holy Spirit. He would not have his behavior influenced by others, but would take his stand and be willing to suffer for Jesus' sake. To me, these are clear indications of spiritual growth.

The Christian leader, therefore, should carefully examine himself to identify those characteristics in his life that may interfere with an uncompromising devotion to the Lord Jesus. Then he should be ready to learn from the circumstances through which the Lord might put him. Thereafter, he should continue to grow in perception and in understanding so that, as he comes to the close of life, he may be able out of the richness and fullness of experience and conviction to say to others as Peter did in the last verse of his second epistle: "Grow in grace and in the knowledge of our Lord and Savior, Jesus Christ."